FATHER

A Look into the Heart of God

GERI KELLER

MorningStar Publications

A DIVISION OF MORNINGSTAR FELLOWSHIP CHURCH
P.O. Box 440
Wilkesboro, NC 28697

Father—A Look into the Heart of God
Geri Keller
Copyright © 2004
Second Printing, 2005

International Standard Book Number—1-929371-42-X

Cover Design by Micah Davis

Unless otherwise indicated, Scripture references are from the New International Version.

Table of Contents

Foreword
by Rick Joyner

I first met Geri (pronounced like Gary) and Lilo Keller at a conference in the Emmental Valley of Switzerland in the early 1990s. I had felt a call to Switzerland and jokingly accepted this speaking engagement because I owed so much to this valley, being the birthplace of Swiss cheese. Even though Geri did not speak much English and I did not speak any German, I felt I could communicate with him immediately. His devotion to the Lord was so pure and so steadfast that it was inspiring just to be around him.

After this conference in the Emmental Valley, my wife, Julie, and I went to stay with Geri and Lilo for a few days at their place in Winterthur, which is close to Zurich. I was scheduled to speak at their meeting at "The Riding Hall," a Swiss army stable. I did not know what to expect. When I saw the nearly two thousand young people jammed into the hall, seemingly sitting in every conceivable space, with more energy and zeal for the Lord than I had ever witnessed in Europe, I was inspired. I talked to some of these kids and found that they often drove six hundred kilometers each way to come to those meetings from Germany, Austria, and all over Switzerland.

It was a remarkable meeting and we fell in love with the entire ministry that Geri and Lilo had raised up, not the least of which was Lilo's worship band. It has become known as one of the best, and it is. Even so, above all I saw an uncommon devotion to the Lord in their whole team, as well as those who attended these meetings. I had already spent years ministering in Europe, but had never seen anything with quite the spiritual quality as what was there.

Even though we were only with them a few days, I was sad to leave Geri and Lilo, but I was surprised when Julie cried. When I asked her what was wrong she said that she felt like she was leaving her father. I have to admit that I felt the same way. In spite of the radical nature of their ministry, which was even more so by European standards, Geri was a rock of stability, maturity, wisdom, and strength, which was greater than I have felt around any man or woman of God that I have ever met.

I make this statement very carefully, as I have had the great privilege of meeting and being close to some of the great men and women of our times. I know some who are true spiritual fathers and great ones, but none quite like I have felt in Geri. Swiss people tend to be very mature, wise, and stable. I feel this to a degree with many Swiss leaders, but what we felt with Geri was far more than could be explained in the natural. John wrote in I John 2:13, **"I am writing to you, fathers, because you know Him who has been from the beginning"** (NAS). Geri has known the Father in a very special way and it exudes from him whether he is speaking or just sitting in front of the fire. This is a remarkable and very rare gift.

Foreword by Rick Joyner

When I heard that Geri had written this book, I knew it was important. When I read it, I was not disappointed. I think the instruction in this book is powerful, but I think its purpose is more than that. This is an impartation of one of the most important ministries on earth. As the apostle Paul lamented, we have many teachers but not many fathers (see I Corinthians 4:15). I think this is true and is one of the greatest weaknesses in the church of our times as well.

The ones we often call fathers are usually older men who have been faithful and have the wisdom of their age, but that is not what qualifies one as a father. To be a father you have to reproduce. In fact, most reproduce when they are younger and often are not very wise yet. There are some ministries that are truly fathers, but they are very rare. Even more rare are those who have wisdom and stability combined with courage to keep going forward, to keep pressing back the limits of our time.

As I heard one friend of mine say, "Being a father is the highest calling of all because it is the one office on this earth that we can share with the Father." For the last thirty plus years the very institution of being a father seems to have been under the most unrelenting assault by the evil one. With but very rare exceptions, almost every father character on television or in the movies is either evil or mentally and socially challenged, to be generous. The question we need to be asking is whether this is a major cause of the breakdown happening now in families or is it just reflecting the true state of things. In truth, there seems to be very few fathers who deserve this high title.

We now seem to hear continually that we are in "a fatherless generation." If this is true, it is because we do not know the

Father the way we should. I am so thankful to have the relationship we have with Geri. I am also very thankful that he has written this book to share what may well be some of the crucial truths that are needed at this time. Even more, I am happy that this book as well as Geri's life points to the Father, not just principles. This is not just about taking our position in a family and doing it right—it is about seeing the glory of God, the Father, and being changed by His glory into His same image.

Many Christians have the concept of the Father as being the God of the Old Testament, the God of the Law, and if it were not for Jesus, He would have destroyed us all. However, we forget that it was the Father who so loved the world that He gave His only Son for our salvation. Our Father loves us that much! He is severe, but He is severe because He loves us so much, not because He is intolerant or impatient.

The Father is just and righteous and He demands both from His children. He is also love, which is the foundation of His justice and His righteousness. This is something I think Geri has seen maybe better than anyone I know, and he imparts it with a grace that can heal the wounded heart, or melt the hardened one.

Preface

It is a great joy to publish this book by Geri Keller, a glimpse into the heart of God and His all-encompassing Fatherhood.

The book contains a collection of sermons that Geri Keller preached to audiences in Switzerland, Austria, and Germany. For the reader, the following points may be helpful.

Originally, each chapter's message was designed to stand alone, but it goes without saying that only the whole spectrum of messages will unfold the wide range of the topic. Thus, there are some repetitions which we did not omit because they highlight the importance of certain aspects.

It is our deepest desire that the reader may be blessed with a fresh vision of the heart of God—the marvelous Father's heart that is longing for each and every one of us.

Schleife Publishing
MorningStar Publications

Introduction
by Geri Keller

I neither planned nor wrote this book, at least not in the way you would normally imagine. My friends at Schleife Publishing just put the finished manuscript into my hands one day. It was shocking; they might as well have placed a baby into my arms, for which I was suddenly supposed to take responsibility. After I worked through my conflicting emotions, the two of us managed to get acquainted and gradually, grew closer.

The statements and phrases, taken from messages I had delivered in the recent past, were certainly familiar to me. In reading them, I relived the circumstances and birth pains which had brought them into being. I became aware that the most important aspect of this book is not merely that it details a certain segment of my life, but that it is the major theme and focus of my very existence.

This was already apparent at my birth. My mother was fighting a seemingly hopeless battle on the delivery bed. I refused and refused to come out and the doctor was, for some reason, nowhere to be found. When he finally appeared, sizing up the situation with a single glance, he jumped onto the table and used his knees to push me out into the daylight. What became visible was a blue and nearly lifeless being, with the umbilical cord wrapped tightly around my neck.

Quickly, the doctor grabbed me by the feet and whirled me around in circles until I produced my first cry. It was not until much later that this experience came to my mind while reading Psalm 22:9: **"But You are He who took Me out of the womb; You made me trust while on My mother's breasts"** (NKJV).

The next verse of this Psalm also shows how God's predetermined plan was coming to pass during my entire childhood and youth: **"I was cast upon You from birth…You have been My God" (Psalm 22:10 NKJV).** Although my parents continually prayed for me, I was mostly left on my own to find my way through life. During that time, I experienced an overwhelming sense of the Fatherhood of God. He took me by the hand and in His sovereign way, encouraged and built me up. This gave me an unshakable foundation of trust in Him. My life has been like a train on a predetermined track, which carried me safely through all the hindrances and detours that tried to come against my calling. One example is the story of "my" crucifix.

As a youth, I took voice lessons from a well-known singer of oratorios. Above his grand piano hung the body of Christ carved out of wood. This crucifix burned an indelible impression into my heart—I saw it as an expression of the love of the Father. Over time, the desire to own such a picture of Jesus myself became stronger and stronger. Finally, I saw a carving similar to the one I had been dreaming of in an antique shop in Zurich. I do not know how long I stood at that window, taking in the sight of the figure of Christ. In a daze, I walked home.

Thankfully, our summer break was about to start and this provided a chance to find work and earn the money I needed to purchase the crucifix. I felt like Jacob while he was working for Rachel, and the time flew by. Before long, I was scurrying down the narrow side streets of the village, but I suddenly began to walk faster when the thought occurred to me: What if the crucifix was no longer there? One look and my heart dropped. The place where the carving had lain was empty. I opened the shop door almost mechanically and the owner must have sensed my deep desperation. Yes, he had sold it he said, but I should come back again in two hours and he would see what he could do.

When I returned to the store, I noticed something wrapped in tissue paper, lying on the table—my Jesus! Now for the first time, I held the carving made by an old farmer from Tirol in my hands. The glazed body suffered from an occasional wormhole and the left, outstretched arm had obviously been broken off and glued back on. There were holes in the hands and feet. Still, to me, everything had been fashioned with gripping simplicity and beauty. When the storeowner gave me a frame for my crucifix, with a velvet background and a real gold border, my happiness was complete. For many years, this image of Jesus would be my companion.

On my father's birthday, I passed my final exams to attain my master's degree in theology. An important period of time had come to a close. Looking back, I can only describe it as a paradise filled with the goodness of Father God.

The next season of my life was like an expedition into the depths of the Father's heart, where I was to discover what **"no eye has seen, no ear has heard, no mind has conceived…"** **(I Corinthians 2:9).** It was about finding the Father, who is greater than all, and whose Fatherhood far surpasses our simplistic notion of a wondrous, protective, glass screen which shields our lives. The sermons collected in this book all revolve around experiences where God presents Himself in

Father

a new and unexpected way every time we encounter Him—greater, holier, more willing to give, more compassionate, and more inconceivable. God just does not match our preconceived ideas! In fact, He is so different that we can only marvel in adoration at the awesome wonder of His Divine Fatherhood.

When I saw the word "FATHER" on the cover of this book, I was shocked at first. I had to look at the title over and over again, sometimes from close up, sometimes from a distance. Although the word was so familiar, the letters appeared foreign and novel, as if I were reading them for the very first time: FATHER!? That may be the reason why we like to add other words to it: our Father, my Father, dear Father, eternal Father. We decided to add a subtitle to the plain word "Father," as well.

This may indeed be an illustration of a deep truth. The word "FATHER" far surpasses our understanding; it is deeply fascinating and yet exceedingly fearsome to us. It is like one of nature's wonders that leaves us speechless. You may try to capture its raw beauty on film, but at the same time you know that the picture will be nothing but a dim reflection. Each and every one of us is a part of it, just like one of the tiny little drops in the mist of Niagara Falls. Oh Father—You are the only hope of the world!

I want to express my deep appreciation for my friends, Ken Janz and Michael Herwig, for their hidden work as gold panners. I dedicate this book to the memory of Jakob Rietmann (1908-2001) from the little town of Herisau in the mountains of Appenzell, a man who became a father and spiritual mentor to many in our nation.

Geri Keller

ONE

Abba, Father

From Counterfeit Fatherhood to the One True Father

Those who are led by the Spirit of God are sons [let me add daughters] **of God.**

For you did not receive a spirit that makes you a slave again to fear, but you received the Spirit of sonship [and of daughterhood]. **And by him we cry, "Abba, Father" (Romans 8:14-15).**

This Aramaic word **"Abba"** is a very affectionate expression for Daddy or Papa—it is something profoundly intimate, flowing from our heart to the heart of the Father. This deep sense of belonging to our heavenly Father can also be found in a well-known passage in Paul's epistle to the Galatians:

But when the fullness of the time came, God sent forth His Son, born of a woman, born under the Law,

so that He might redeem those who were under the Law, that we might receive the adoption as sons [and daughters].

Father

Because you are sons [and daughters], **God has sent forth the Spirit of His Son into our hearts, crying, 'Abba! Father!'**

Therefore you are no longer a slave, but a son [and a daughter]; **and if a son** [and a daughter], **then an heir through God. (Galatians 4:4-7, NAS)**

Deep within all of us, there is a cry for the love of the Father. We are searching for this Father. In one of the songs we sing it says, "Show me Your Father's heart, O God!" This reveals the deep longing, the cry of our heart to be filled. Often we hold certain expectations in our minds and souls of how this should be done: "Just take me into Your arms! Hold me tight, gently rock me, comfort me, caress my hair, and let me feel it!" All too often, when we pray for people they end up being disappointed because things just do not happen the way they expect. Every once in a while those prayers trigger deep feelings of pain that have been locked up inside, and people start screaming, and even powers are expelled. However, what are we actually looking for—what is this love of the Father?

The Struggle for Fatherhood

We are facing a life and death battle! When Jesus came into this world, Satan confronted Him personally. Jesus called him the **"prince of this world"** (see John 14:30). Ultimately, God is Lord over the earth, but Satan used the Fall to claim the right of ownership in this world. He puffs himself up as the father. He is a master of lies, trying to fake fatherhood on many different levels.

Scores of leaders have called themselves "father." Whole nations looked up to these so-called "fathers." Think how many politicians, teachers, professors, and doctors, among others, enjoy taking a posture as fathers! Lies are being spread about what true fatherhood is meant to be. People are being deceived—some are even being abused in the name of fatherhood by psychologists, therapists, clergy, and many others. Because of this, Jesus once said, **"And do not call anyone on earth 'father'"... (Matthew 23:9).**

Yes, we do need spiritual fathers and mothers who are able to share God's heart with us. Yet, we are not to call ourselves fathers and mothers, for there is but one true Father! Regarding this Father, the Bible says in Ephesians 4:6, **"...who is over all and through all and in all."** In Jesus, true and genuine Fatherhood came into our world once again. He said, **"He who has seen Me has seen the Father,"** (John 14:9 NAS) and has seen true Fatherhood, the true heart of the Father.

There is a battle raging for fatherhood. Satan knew that if true fatherhood was revealed in this world, his false fatherhood of lies, deception, humanism, ideologies, perversion, and abuse would be dismantled and he would be doomed. For this very reason a cosmic power struggle erupted. Satan raised the stakes to the highest possible degree when he showed Jesus all the kingdoms of the world in one single glance, saying, **"All these things I will give You, if You fall down and worship me" (Matthew 4:9, NAS).** This power struggle is raging more fiercely than ever today. It is the struggle for this world to come under the true Fatherhood of God. However, for this to be possible, we have to enter into our position as children, again. The spirit of childlikeness is to be poured out on men, women, teenagers, and old people alike.

Father

Here in Nuremberg,[1] the city that saw the spectacular mass gatherings at Nazi party conventions during the Third Reich, this battle flared up with particular ferocity. In this city, the lie of counterfeit fatherhood was expressed and propagated in such a way that uncounted thousands of young people, being totally deceived, were enticed to dedicate their lives to a counterfeit father figure.

Some years ago, during a visit to Nuremberg, I woke up early in the morning in my hotel room thinking I was in China. Barely awake, I was reasoning back and forth—"I don't have any Chinese currency. How shall I pay for the soda water I took out of the refrigerator last night?" Sometime later it finally dawned on me where I really was, "Oh yes, I am in Germany. I do have a few German Marks to pay my room service bill."

I became aware that these moments of confusion were part of a prophetic experience. This is a place of confusion, and this confusion is about the issue of fatherhood! Power encounters between the Father of all Fatherhood and the father of lies causes a tremendous amount of upheaval and disorientation. Wherever this battle is raging, the power of the enemy will surface. When Jesus entered into the synagogues or crossed graveyards, the demons shrieked.

The Birthing of a Child of God

You do not have to be afraid—becoming a child of God always has something to do with birthing. Birth is a process that always involves blood, tears, and pain. There must be labor pains!

---

[1] This message was preached at a conference in Nuremberg.

Abba, Father

Birth is often accompanied by sorrows and misery (even Jesus saw it this way, see John 16:21-22). However, once the birth pains yield their fruit and new life breaks forth, there will be joy!

All of us who are being called by Jesus to come under this heavenly Fatherhood are entering into a birth process. Nobody is exempt! Some go through an easy birth; others suffer a breech birth. Some need to be delivered from their mother's womb through a C-section; others miraculously turn around in the womb and find their natural way out. Finally, there are some that do not even want to come out at all until contractions are being induced through medication. The bottom line is that birth will always be a struggle and we should not be surprised about that. We are talking about spiritual life here, but wherever life is being generated, death is inevitably threatened as well.

It has always been that way in the kingdom of God—wherever Satan, the father of lies celebrates his triumphs, Jesus comes to build His kingdom. The prophets reveal to us, "He is building His kingdom amidst the ancient ruins" (see Isaiah 44:26, 61:4). He breaks forth like a highly condensed stream of water.

Some years ago, 70,000 students gathered in the Olympic arena in Seoul, South Korea. They knelt down on the turf and promised God that they would dedicate themselves to Jesus and devote part of the life and strength of their youth to missions. Kneeling there under the pouring rain, these 70,000 young people proclaimed, "We offer up our lives to You, Jesus. You may use us in any way you want, Lord!" Today, we ask God to restore to us what was lost to counterfeit fatherhood many years ago in Nuremberg. Much reconciliation has already taken place, and spiritual life has welled up again in this city, but we pray for an army of young people to rise up under the banner of the true Father of all Fatherhood.

The baby in the womb has no idea of the bigger picture; it does not even know how to say "Mom" or "Dad" and yet it was conceived from its father and is being nourished by its mother. It is connected to the life-supporting blood vessels of a female body. At the given time this life breaks forth, but still the baby is unable to say "Mom" or "Dad." Its only utterance is a scream as it passes into the realm of light, and air penetrates its little lungs for the first time. It has a long way to go until it is capable of recognizing father and mother as the faces that are bending over the cradle to look into its eyes.

We have the notion that spiritual birth is something instant, like microwave popcorn. However, God makes it quite clear: **"Ask and it will be given to you; seek and you will find; knock and the door will be opened to you" (Matthew 7:7).**

God is taking us on a journey that requires our active participation! He is a creative God, and we are to seek, knock, and slowly grope our way. Think about little toddlers. They pick up everything and stick it in their mouths. That is how they feel their way around the world. The same is true in the spiritual realm. We must get to know the world of God by feeling our way into it: Who is this God, Creator of the universe? Why did He lead Abraham out to show him the starry sky? Why did Jesus say, **"Look at the birds of the air!... Consider the lilies of the field...?" (Matthew 6:26-28, NKJV)** Why does this marvelous creation exist? Go out and take a look at the amazing bounty of His works and say, "My Father made all of this!" It may not solve all of your problems, but it will surely help you to get to know your heavenly Father in a deeper way."

So, we learn and feel our way closer to Him, who tenderly turns to us, saying, "It's Me, My son, My daughter. I made all of this—I made it for you, in order to give you an abundance of life, in order to give you a tiny hint how I feel about you and what I would like to tell you! My heart is so much bigger, and My love for you is boundless!"

There are a thousand different ways in which God helps us to become aware of Himself as our Father. It is not about a quick fix experience; He wants to slowly awaken our senses to the beauties of His Fatherhood. I have already experienced a lot of it. It is all over me, with me, in me. And yet I am still searching, knocking, asking, because I know that I have not even begun to tap into the vastness of His Father's heart. "Show me Your Father's heart, O God!" This is my desire, my deepest yearning.

Grace Is the Key

Oftentimes, we are confronted with our own inability to receive the love and the character of God. In Jesus, the true image of the Father came into the world. In the gospel of John we read that He is **"full of grace and truth" (John 1:14 NAS). "Grace and truth"** are part of God's character. First and foremost, God is gracious, compassionate, and full of mercy. It is extremely difficult for us to accept the grace of God. I can almost hear the objections welling up now that the grace of God is all too often made a "cheap grace." However, it seems to me that we sometimes speak of "cheap grace" because we have not yet taken hold of grace to its fullest extent and are still heeding the prideful notion in our hearts that we must somehow contribute to it and earn it. Grace is grace!

Father

Both grace and truth were revealed in the cross. The message of the cross is this: You cannot come close to the Father's heart by any means except through grace. You cannot earn the Father's love, you cannot accumulate it through rigorous Bible study, you cannot pray it in, nothing you do whatsoever can give you access to it. Through grace, it is already yours. This is more than we can handle! For this reason, the cross is so offensive. We want to contribute something—even if it may only be the prospect of a reincarnation so that we can atone for our misdeeds in a future life.

We can see this attitude in the Pharisee in the temple who boasted, **"I fast twice a week; I pay tithes of all that I get"** **(Luke 18:12 NAS)** and "I go to pray three times a day!" At the same time, there was a desolate man, a tax collector, a totally corrupt person who finally gave it a try to get right with God. He had sneaked through the back door into the temple in order to express his longing for the Father's heart. As he overheard the things the Pharisee said, he became totally discouraged. Finally, he said to himself, "There's just no way for me! Fasting twice a week…" He thought of his full refrigerator at home, the many invitations he had to attend, and all of the business lunches with his fellow tax collectors. "Praying three times a day, paying tithes of everything I get…" Then he beat his breast and said, **"God, be merciful to me, the sinner" (Luke 18:13 NAS).**

What Jesus wanted to convey to us is this: If such a person beats his breast, saying, "God, have mercy on me!", if somebody out of the depths of his affliction cries out to God, He will hear him and assure him of His grace.

Jesus made it very clear: "Whoever will call on Me will be saved" (see Romans 10:13). It is one of the most difficult things to accept the grace of God. We always want to do something in order to earn it; we want to pay for it, to give something in return just so it would not be for free anymore. Yet, it is for free! God says, "I will be gracious to whom I will be gracious. It is My decision to whom I want to show mercy, not yours. I decide to whom I will show compassion; it is none of your business" (see Exodus 33:19).

Many years ago, I came to a point where I felt I had to quit being a pastor immediately. I said to myself, "The Lord will never be able to use a jerk like me. This is it!" I wrote my notice to the district board, dropped the keys to the church in the mailbox, loaded my old sofa and some boxes full of books into my car, and drove off to Zurich, where I moved into a small, furnished room. I just knew it was over, once and for all. I knew I would never be in ministry again. Never! I tried a couple of other things. I wanted to drive a taxicab, but I failed the exam. I took a few classes in remedial education, worked at a television station shooting movies, and finally became a nurse's assistant in a psychiatric hospital. In order to punish myself a little, I chose to work on closed wards. Later, I agreed to live together with the patients in an open ward for months. I even lived in a special unit for patients with tuberculosis for a while. I exhausted myself totally for them because I did not care about my own future anymore.

However, God did not give in to my attempts to get away from Him. He said: "The only lesson you need to learn is grace. You cannot earn My grace. And if I have decided to use someone like you, if I want you as My son, that's My decision, not yours!" But there was still too much pride left inside of me. Not only did I want to contribute to my redemption and to my salvation, there was also a side of me that still wanted to boast. After all, I had a fairly clean slate. "Not like this fellow over there!" said the Pharisee. "God, I thank you that I am not like the evildoers, tax collectors, or adulterers" (see Luke 18:11).

After I had wrestled for three years, I finally came to the point where I said, "Okay, Lord, I surrender. I accept Your grace." From this time on, I started to sense His Father's heart again. I felt Him putting His arm around me saying, "You could have had this without going through all the hassle. I have loved you with an everlasting love. With lovingkindness, I have drawn you. I do not love you because you are a neat guy, because you attracted large crowds to your church, or because you lived a morally pure life. The reason I love you is because I made up My mind to love you!"

God chose us before the foundation of the world, before we even existed. Just to make it very clear, "God demonstrated His love for us while we were still His enemies, when we were still sinners." (see Romans 5:8-10). He already loved you back then! God gave Himself in Jesus to bear all of the guilt and sin and sickness of the world. When Jesus came to display His wounds to the disciples, God demonstrated to us beyond a shadow of a doubt: "I have chosen you, even if that involved facing the cross in order to take care of your sin!"

Grace and Truth

We will never be able to earn this incredible grace of God. We can only receive it as a gift. Nevertheless, there is still so much pride lingering inside of us. We are performance-driven, feeling as if we have to achieve something so we do not have to depend wholly on the grace of God. Yet, we have to—there is no other way! And for this very reason, Christ is **"full of grace"** while at the same time being "full of truth" (see John 1:14).

As Jesus was hanging on the cross, He became sin and took upon Himself the curse for the whole world; He took your sin as well as mine, He took our sicknesses, our personal backgrounds, and the bitter roots of our heart. He also took the sins of cities and nations, as well as the burden of history, all of the appalling horrors of the past. It is the truth: He carried it, and thus we do not have to carry it anymore. Whoever is searching for Him will not be punished for sin anymore: **"the punishment that brought us peace was upon him"** (Isaiah 53:5).

As Christians, we will be a people of transparency who have no need to cover up or pretend anything. We do not have to hide behind masks—we are who we are. Jesus in us is enough, and the Holy Spirit within us will transform us into His image. We are genuine!

Some time ago, there was a large Christian gathering in the city of Basel, Switzerland with about 10,000 people in attendance. During that meeting, there was a panel discussion involving a group of nationally recognized, spiritual leaders. One of them was a very well known leader of a significant spiritual movement in Switzerland. All of the participants had received a certain book well in advance in order to prepare them for the topic of the discussion.

In the beginning, we were asked what had come to our minds when we read the book. This particular leader's turn came and he said, "Well, I must admit that I haven't read the book." He did not hide in the bathroom a couple of minutes before the meeting in order to go over the summary. He did not flip through

Father

Christian magazines on his way to the meeting to see if he could find a book report and pretend he had read it. He had the guts to admit before an audience of 10,000 watching him on giant screens: "Well, I haven't read the book." Hallelujah! This man really took a bold stand for Christ on that podium.

We live by grace, and we love truth. In other words: I am acceptable, not because I do well or never forget anything or because I am always prepared. I live by grace and by the power of the Holy Spirit who helps me every day to step out in obedience. In the midst of it all, truth is our only protection. If the world sees us living by truth—not yielding to falsehood, but clinging to truthfulness—this will make us witnesses beyond anything else we could do for God. God loves you as you take a stand for truth.

2

The Fatherhood of God

Our Only Safe Place

If I want to break through to the knowledge of His Fatherhood, I need to be willing to become a child! A child is dependent on its father. By requiring that we become childlike, Jesus opened up a gigantic front in the battle against the world and its cultural values. He made it very plain that **"unless you change and become like little children, you will never enter the kingdom of heaven" (Matthew 18:3).**

Children are not enslaved by the power of mammon. They live in the present moment. They are wholly dependent on their father and mother or their provider. They are unable to take charge of their lives and provide for themselves. Jesus came and proclaimed: "Do you desire to become children once again? Are you willing to depend on your heavenly Father so He can enter into His role as the One who is in charge of your life and be your Provider?"

Our world is based on security. For this very reason we see enormous struggles for the resources in our society. There are raging battles over little fractions of a percent in government subsidies, over budget cuts for welfare programs, and about who is eligible for special assistance funds or who is not. Everything is based on security; it is the very foundation of our life.

However, our only true security is the Fatherhood of God! Again the question is: "Are you willing to become a child again and enter into a position of total dependence upon your heavenly Father, where you may still keep your worldly securities (thank God for them!), but you are not ultimately dependent on them?"

Much of the body of Christ is still bound by mammon—the mammon of security. As Christians, we are no less fighting for our share and over fractions of a percent in church taxes. We are fighting for positions and privileges because they represent a form of security. Jesus said to Peter, **"Come!"** and Peter got out of his boat and stepped on the water (see Matthew 14:29). Whoever tries to walk on water will inevitably get to swallow some and cry out to Jesus for help. Yet, each time He will stretch out His hand toward you, pull you out of the water, and say, **"O you of little faith, why did you doubt?" (Matthew 14:31 NKJV).**

Happiness Is Dependence on God

There is no greater form of happiness than dependence upon God. Certainly, this way of life has its own challenges. Over and over again, God is a "last minute" God. Oftentimes we assume God may be overly punctual and help us out a week or two in advance in order to relieve our anxious hearts. But this is just not God's way, although at times He may come a little in advance in order to build up our faith. Moses was on his way through the wilderness with millions of people and all of their cattle. They had not found any water for three days! As they came to a little waterhole, everybody ran to quench his thirst, but those who tried the water spat it out in disgust because it was undrinkable and poisonous (see Exodus 15:22-24). God, what are You doing here?

Once we are dependent upon God, life becomes overwhelmingly thrilling! God wants us to come out of our everyday boredom. The Swabian motto, "Never rest! Never rest! Keep building your nest," cannot be all there is to life. There must be more to it. As the Quakers said, "Christians are incredibly happy, absolutely fearless, and always in trouble." You may go through times of deep frustration and total disorientation. You may moan and groan and cry out to God, saying, "Father, I have no clue where to go from here! What are You doing to me?"

God is our heavenly Father, and He does not allow you to go through rough times just because He is so busy that He totally forgot about you. He wants to deepen your confidence in Him. What did the Pharisees and teachers of the law say while Jesus was dying on the cross? **"He trusted in God; let Him deliver Him now" (Matthew 27:43, NKJV).** This is the most wonderful compliment anyone could ever make to Jesus: **"He trusted in God."** If there is anything we could honor God with, it is childlike trust in Him as our heavenly Father.

We must become totally dependent on God. Often, His plans vary from our own. He may want to lead us on a different road. We are involved in an astounding process where we learn to make room for God in our lives. Time and again we need to ask and closely listen as we say, "God, what now? Where shall I go from here?" We are not the ones performing the great miracles; we are just contributing some fishes and a few loaves of bread.

Father

We may prepare the dough or lay a foundation, anoint sick people with oil, lay hands on them, and speak the Word of God over them, but He is doing the actual job.

We are about to enter a most exciting time—when we become children. We will allow ourselves to be ignorant once again, constantly bombarding the Father with our questions, "Father, what now? Where do we go from here?" We are about to enter a time where we will no longer vote among the elders as to whether we want to hold a certain seminar, extend the Sunday morning worship time by ten minutes, or whether the youth should be allowed a little more freedom in dealing with the Holy Spirit—all this is over with!

When we have His Spirit in us, He prompts us to call out **"Abba, Father!"** over and over again, pleading with Him, "Father, we need to know what to do right now. Please tell us!" We cannot just stick to the old ways. Our God is a creative God. Each new day, He goes on to a different place. Jesus often turned around and asked His disciples, "Do you still want to follow Me, or do you want to leave?" (see John 6:67).

The road goes on and on toward the final goal, where God becomes Father over this world once again. His children, in whom He delights, are to return to Him. He wants to pour out His lovingkindness in place of the injustice, callousness, and cruelty that rules the world today. Truth is to replace lies. In a Christian community, there is to be a sharing of hearts without abuse or control.

It is true: God is moving on, and we need to be children in order to accept and embrace such a total dependence on Him. We will always be children. We may be the most powerful and

The Fatherhood of God

most anointed men and women of God, and yet we always remain in this position of total dependence, where we keep calling out to Him, **"Abba, Father!"** There is no other way; we have to keep coming back to the Father, staying in His presence and crying on His shoulder: "Father, I just can't go on; I feel like quitting!" Then He will say to us: "Oh, you little silly-billy, I am your heavenly Father. I am bigger than anything else. No one can pluck you out of My hand! I am about to do something new in your life. The old has passed away! I just allowed a few stitches to slip because I want to change the pattern. I am starting a new section in the pattern of your life."

I am so thrilled about my God, although it may be a strain to follow Him and even a little painful at times—but nevertheless it is a life so marvelously beautiful and glorious! Paul says, **"Everywhere and in all things I have learned both to be full and to be hungry, both to abound and to suffer need. I can do all things through Christ who strengthens me" (Philippians 4:12-13 NKJV).** This is only possible because we have a Father who is **"greater than all" (John 10:29).**

I would like for you to get to a point where you make a new promise to your God, saying: "Yes, Lord, I am willing to take this position as a child, once again. I am willing to leave my independence behind, in the way You would have me to, and to quit keeping every domain of my life under my own control. Wherever I have already made up my mind how I want to spend the coming years of my life, and what direction my marriage and my family should take—I surrender all of that to You. God, I am willing to become dependent on You. I resist mammon; I resist false notions of power; I accept the position as a dependent child, and I want to be built up as a son and a daughter of my heavenly Father."

Father

Children—the Greatest Threat to Satan

Children are the most dangerous thing for the world and for Satan. For this reason, he tries all he can to force children to become like adults as early as possible. Once they are adults, they need securities, they need to know where the "next fix" will come from. Thus, he attempts to rob us of our childhood and to turn us into adults prematurely—independent, self-made, so-called self-sufficient individuals who, in reality, are poor and desperate. This fake adulthood has become the foundation of our society, and the devil fears nothing more than a childlike people of sons and daughters of God.

I am so excited that the Lord is building up a children's movement worldwide: be it "King's Kids" or be it radical teenagers who are willing to advance in total dependence upon God. The Lord is setting up a sign once more, even to us adults, that His desire is for us to become dependent and to radically put our trust in Him.

Prayer

Father, Abba, Father! I want to thank You for all those who have been created by You in their innermost being and for those who are still to be created—not by the seed of a man, not by blind passion, not by lust; they are being formed by You, out of the heart of a Father, out of the boundless passion of Your Father's heart. I thank You for all of the birthing processes that are going on right now in our lives. Thank You for everybody who has already tasted and seen Your Fatherhood. Thank You as well for those who are still searching, and who are slowly feeling their way towards You.

To those I pronounce a blessing over you, that you may stay on this path and would not be distracted from searching, asking, and

The Fatherhood of God

knocking. It is the Father Himself who has been searching for you for generations past. The Father has chosen you, and His only desire is to draw you close to His heart and reveal His heart to you.

I thank you, Jesus, that You will advance us further in this process. We will taste and feel; we will allow the name of the Father to melt on our tongues like a precious delicacy—like honey on our lips. Lord, would You put this sweet name of the Father right into our spirits and into our hearts again? Let the name of Abba melt once again in our hearts and in our spirits. Call it out into our hearts and into our spirits: Abba! Abba! He is your Abba! Your Abba!

I thank You Lord, that You will convict us in areas where we are still bound by pride and unable to receive You as Abba, in Your love and Your grace. Convict us where we are still looking into the mirror, asking ourselves: "May I do this? Will I be able to do that? What else can I bring to God in my own strength?" Father I pray for a release. Enable us to open our hearts and receive Your grace. May a stream of grace be released, today.

I also pray for a release to step out of our reserved attitudes. I pray for a release to open up areas where we hold back, where we cover up and repress painful things in our lives. I pray for a release to step out into the light of truth, for we are called to be men and women of God, with our rough edges and imperfections—people who are not perfect, but who are transparent. Thus, the light of Christ can pass through them for everybody else to see and be utterly amazed: Those are ordinary people, just like us, but there is peace in them—what a peace!

I honor You for all of this, Father.

THREE

Like a Father
Jesus, the Only Access

"As a father has compassion on his children, so the Lord has compassion on those who fear him" (Psalm 103:13).

The Allegory of Fatherhood and Motherhood

Earthly concepts of fatherhood and motherhood are used as allegories in the Bible. We can only grasp eternal and heavenly realities through images and ideas reflected in this world. Yet, these are imperfect aids. God always uses them with a certain reservation because any earthly image can only be a flawed representation of His perfect character. Thus He says in Isaiah, **"Can a mother forget the baby at her breast and have no compassion on the child she has borne?"** But then He quickly adds, **"Though she may forget, I will not forget you!"** (Isaiah 49:15).

Through the prophet Isaiah, God introduced Himself as our **"Everlasting Father"** (Isaiah 9:6). It is His character to be the Father, and His character is immutable. God does not grow out of His status as Father by becoming a Grandfather, and later maybe a Great-Grandfather; God is a Father through and through, a Father par excellence. He is the **"Everlasting Father:"** from eternity to eternity, He has been and will always be Father. For this very reason, Paul bends his knees before **"...the Father, from whom his whole family in heaven and on earth derives its name" (Ephesians 3:14-15).** Luther translated this "the Father who is the true Father over all who are being called children in heaven and on earth."

Deep in his heart, Paul had come to an understanding of the Father's heart in this God who had met him in a very special way. God had led him out of bondage from self-justice, religious pride, arrogance, and presumptuousness against his Creator, and had made him an apostle to the nations. Over and over again, Paul sang the praises of the eternal Fatherhood of his God. There is not a single one of his letters where he did not use expressions like **"Grace and peace to you from God our Father and the Lord Jesus Christ"(I Corinthians 1:3).** Peace from God our Father—this is not merely a liturgical expression; it is based upon the intimate, personal knowledge of one who himself had found peace in God's eternal Fatherhood. Thus he is able to say, "For I am convinced that nothing—nothing ever—will be able to separate us from the love of God that is in Christ Jesus our Lord" (see Romans 8:38-39).

For this very reason, feelings of helplessness tend to overcome me whenever I have to preach about this **"Everlasting Father."** We look to earthly fathers in order to somehow grasp who God is, and we should do so. In a time where an epidemic of fatherlessness has run rampant, God may support us through spiritual mothers and fathers. For a season, they are supposed to guide us to the heart of the Father through Jesus Christ.

With their help, we learn the first lessons of what fatherhood can really mean. How can I understand what a father is unless I have experienced fathering? When I am suddenly facing the giant ocean of God's Fatherhood and find myself diving into this vast secret, I also feel like the miners, which I read about in the newspaper recently who had been trapped in a collapsed mining tunnel. Having spent more than ten days in total darkness, they had to be blindfolded after their rescue because they could not stand the light of day.

Paul was literally blinded by the reality of God's Fatherhood. God in His wisdom decreed that this knowledgeable and enlightened man, this genius of a biblical scholar, be blinded by God's Fatherhood in Christ. Paul fell off his horse and could not see for three days, until brother Ananias came, laid hands on him, and said, "Brother Saul, you may see again" (see Acts 9:17).

Jesus—the Only Way to the Father

It is impossible to grasp the reality of Fatherhood. Not even in eternity, when we will be standing before the throne of God the Father, and He will be **"…all in all" (I Corinthians 15:28)**, will we be able to fully comprehend it. Let me make it quite clear though: There is no other way to the Father except through Jesus. Only in Jesus is it possible for us to come to a knowledge of the Father and to break through to His love.

On the other hand, Jesus said, **"No one can come to me unless the Father who sent me draws him" (John 6:44).** Every yearning in you, every hunger, every unrest, every cry of your heart—whatever drove you over all those years when you were still in bondage to sin, living in adultery or fornication, serving foreign gods—every bit of longing in you, the unrest that weighed you down in desperation, and all kinds of addictions— In all of this you could sense the Father drawing you. Nothing else will bring us to Jesus, except for this feeling of homesickness that results from the Father's knocking at the door of our heart, pulling us toward Him.

Only through Jesus can we come to the Father. The blood of His devotion cleanses us from all sin, and then Jesus can take us with Him to the Father. The first person He took to the Father was the delinquent who was hanging on the cross next to Him. This man did not have time to confess his sins in more detail, let alone to lead a righteous life after his conversion. He only said, "I know I am getting what I deserve. **"Jesus, remember me when You come into Your kingdom"** (see Luke 23:41-43).

Think about it: The first saved person to enter into the Father's kingdom together with Jesus was a criminal! He was not an apostle, nor a mighty anointed evangelist, nor a prophet! He was not a seasoned man or woman of God who had lived a life of sacrifice for Him. He brought a miserable, old felon bearing the same wounds from the crucifixion as He Himself wore. He presented that newly redeemed creature to the Father, saying: "Father, here is My brother, Your child; I bring him to You, straight from the cross!" That is awesome! We can only come to the Father through Jesus.

The Old Testament describes how David gathered to himself in the desert the most pathetic company you could imagine: criminals, thieves, outcasts, and all kinds of people who could not make it in life or who were at odds with society. All of these wild men went into the desert to join David. He made them his friends and brothers. Criminals, outcasts, rebels, and ruthless anarchists became his heroes whose names are noted forever, one by one, and remembered in Israel. To this day, they hold a place of honor in the Bible, these mighty men of God who became pillars in the great Davidic kingdom, a prophetic precursor of the eternal kingdom of God. David built it on the shoulders of men like these.

With Jesus at our side, we can always come to the Father. Jesus says, "Look, Father—here is My brother, My sister, here is My friend!" We confess our sins because Jesus lives in us and it is a pleasure and a privilege to become His friends. We want to become like Him and we sense that He does not care as much about our sins as He does about leading us to the Father.

It is our desire to lead the world to Jesus, but we can only win the hearts of sinners if we are no longer bound by sin. This is a paradox: there are many who want to keep one foot in the world, thinking, "I want to remain friends with the world, just to keep the doors open, so I can relate to people outside." That is false logic. Thousands followed Jesus; the head tax collector sat in a tree in order to cast a glance at Him! (see Luke 19:1-4) One of the disciples was a tax collector, and another one was a zealot, a rioter. What caused them to seek the company of Jesus? How could all of these tax collectors invite Him to their parties, and even have a lot of fun with Him? How could people in Cana celebrate a wedding with such exuberance that they did not even notice when they ran out of wine? (see John 2:1-3) There is only one explanation: Jesus was pure.

Only the Pure can Accept the Sinner

"To the pure, all things are pure…" (Titus 1:15). Only the pure are capable of accepting sinners in such a way that they no longer see the sin in them, primarily knowing them to be created by their loving Creator, true children of their eternal Father for whom Jesus died on the cross. They hear the cry of the Father until these lost ones come home to His heart. For this very reason, sinners, adulterers, and tax collectors flocked to Jesus in masses. He was pure and without sin! And because we are still so stained and burdened with sin, people who come to church today sometimes have a hard time. Because we have sin in our lives, we see the sin in others, instead of seeing God's creation. Jesus wanted to point this out when He described how we focus on the "splinters in the eyes of others" because we have a "log in our own eye" (see Matthew 7:3). It is my own impurity which leads me to zero in on the impurities I see in others.

One thing is astonishing—as soon as we are cleansed by the blood of Jesus, and come to the light just the way we are, no longer trying to cover up whatever is deficient and wounded (what is yet to be redeemed)—we will see people come to us. They will be unbelievers, people who are literally coming from the gutter, as well as respected businessmen, doctors, and scholars.

Why did God train Joseph, a young man with lofty dreams, full of pride and self-justice, through years of imprisonment? His father and mother and all of his brothers were to bow before him—sun, moon, and stars were to revolve around him! These dreams were not just phony reveries, they were authentic prophetic revelations, but God had to purify Joseph of his pride. So he served, was imprisoned unjustly, and had to wait on others.

First, he became a slave in the house of Potiphar, cleaning toilets without any compensation—nothing. And yet this prepared him to become a father figure to Pharaoh because he could accept Pharaoh for the king that he was. Pharaoh sensed something in him: This man did not just see everything in Egypt that was not compliant with his Hebrew culture, or with the ways of his religion. Joseph was able to see beyond the mask of Pharaoh, into the heart of a man who cared about the future of his people. He knew that "God is the God of the Egyptians just as much as He is the God of my fathers. There is only one Eternal Father who is also the God and Father of Pharaoh."

This is the way men like Daniel and Joseph became fathers. Awesome kings and emperors, leaders of the mightiest nations of their times asked for their counsel. Why? Because sin no longer had a part in these men of God. We need churches today that are not hypocritical, that are not legalistic, but are fellowships of people who are being touched and transformed by Jesus Christ and are not under the dominion of sin anymore. As a result, they can receive every sinner who comes to church with authentic joy. They do not check him out and scrutinize him first. They do not ask themselves, "Who's this weird stranger? What's he up to?"

That was the secret of William Booth, the General of the Salvation Army. He was a man who continued to live in the fire of his first love, knowing the power of the blood of Jesus. This knowledge drove him onto the streets, and people were drawn to him like flies. Soon after, they put on a uniform themselves, took their instruments and praised Jesus on other streets, amidst the misery of alcoholism running rampant at that time.

Sin Chokes Life

We can only come to the Father through Jesus. In the process, we confess our sins. But the primary focus is life, not sin! Sin always causes death. Even the most insignificant sin, anything that is somehow at odds with the ways of God, chokes life! We are not dealing with a question of morals here. Church is not about moral issues. We have preached moralism for too long, and people turned away from us.

We do not want to encourage people to become nice and well-behaved, let alone to become boring. Some time ago, a pastor told me about a teenager who attended his one-year preparation class which was required for confirmation. One day he wrote with chalk on a pew, "Somebody got bored to death here!" and left, never to be seen in church again. What a shame! Church is supposed to be a place of life.

There is pain, sorrow, and tears involved when we confess our sins. Sometimes it is deeply painful to wrestle with surfacing feelings of shame, but we will become much happier and more joyful as we confess the sin in our lives. Is there not a sense of excitement and fresh expectation? Do we not enjoy a new perspective and restored relationships? All this together is called life! God hates sin so much because it destroys life. It is the **"father of lies" (John 8:44)** who wants to make us believe that God was not willing to grant us true life. That is nonsense!

The life the world has to offer can be compared to dope. It feels like it would invigorate and empower us to gain pleasure, fame, medals, and to make a name for ourselves, but in the end it leaves us with shame and regrets. Every sin must be paid for. You may pay for it with the health of your body or soul, with your relationships, or the well-being of your spirit—or you may let Jesus pay for it. On the cross, Jesus paid for all of your sins so you do not have to pay for them anymore. He took the penalty upon Himself. Only through Him can we come to the Father.

Knowing God

Sometimes it happens that God just touches someone with His Father's love because He is so overwhelmed and unable to contain Himself any longer. But do we know how long a cry had been confined in the depth of that person's heart? How long could the journey have been until this person eventually realized that the Father was there to meet him? Then his heart, soul, and spirit could finally start rejoicing, "I have arrived at my Father's house!"

The gospel makes it very clear: Love means to be "known." It is not just something you experience, although experience is part of it, but love cannot exist without "knowing." Therefore sex, without this aspect of knowing, is a lie. It has death in it. The Bible teaches that a man and a woman will "know" each other as they give themselves to one another. We do not exploit our partner, we are not objects of lust that are easily available to one another for a sensual experience, but we "know" each other for who we really are—deep in our hearts. In the process, we travel a little further down the path of unveiling the secret of who this person really is and get to "know" him or her on a deeper level.

For more than thirty years, Jesus learned obedience and submission. At the same time, He "knew" the Father. By the age of twelve, when He was in the temple, we can see that He already had a perception of the Father, and every time Jesus searched for Him, this knowledge of His Father's heart grew. Antoine de Saint-Exupéry expressed this process so well in his book, *The Little Prince*, when the little prince said to the fox: *"You and I need to travel some distance together, we need to get to 'know' each other and discover who you are and who I am."*

This journey of realizing and recognizing those around us really is a marvelous process. It has its beginnings in the mother's womb where we start picking up the blessings of our parents and thus receive a first impression of who this Father is. It is a beautiful progression in which our knowledge slowly expands, and it will never stop increasing until we finally proceed from believing to seeing, knowing God the way He knows us. There is a very special aspect about God's love—He already knows you like no psychologist ever will. No psychological test, no psychoanalysis, no refined computer assessment method could ever investigate the depths of your heart like God does. Only He is able to really know you because He created you.

As a young boy, I loved to watch how calves were taught to suckle. Usually this was the job of the farmer's wife. It is tough to get these impetuous creatures to finally dig their nose into the drinking fountain. You receive a good drenching until you finally get your fingers in their mouth, causing them to start sucking. It takes a lot of effort to teach calves to suckle! You see the same thing with babies. When they are hungry and you put them to the breast, it may take them a while to realize that they need to suck, not bite.

Oftentimes we act just as clumsily in our relationship with the Father in heaven. That is why we need the Holy Spirit. Getting to know someone is a journey, and only the grace of God makes it possible that a touch of the Father's love even reaches you. It is His marvelous grace! God wants to draw you close to His heart, teach you who He is, and what His eternal Fatherhood means. The more your heart breaks free from the burdens of your past, the more your spirit is released to get to know Him because it is no longer bound to the soul that keeps sending out its confusing false messages.

FOUR

Eternal Father

The Primary Basis of Trust

Eternal Father! When Jesus came with the gospel of redemption, His intention was to bring us back to the Father's house and restore the Father to us. We are in need of the Father. Without Him we cannot live—neither in this age, nor in eternity. Here we are on this rotating planet, amidst a vast universe we cannot even begin to fathom. We cannot add a tiny bit to our life span, even if we deep-freeze our dead body. How do you expect to stand firm in a world that is going through incredibly radical changes at an ever-increasing speed?

We are being misled to believe that things will ultimately turn out well and that the world will become a safer place. The opposite is true. Things are only getting worse. We sometimes celebrate the weather forecast on the evening news like a liturgy. The meteorologists are our "prophets" who point out on a map the expected depressions and weather fronts. An air of certainty surrounds them and they present the forecast very much like the gospel was preached in former times, and we tend to be naïve enough to believe this delusion of security.

Father

Joshua once said, **"O sun, stand still over Gibeon, O moon, over the Valley of Aijalon" (Joshua 10:12).** No weather forecast predicted that the sun would stand still and a whole day would go missing from the calendar. We might believe this is a legend, but it is the truth, just like it is true that a violent earthquake took place the moment Jesus died on the cross. Graves opened and people who had died appeared in Jerusalem. Another earthquake happened on the day of the resurrection, as if to wake up Jesus from the dead so He would put His pierced feet on this earth once again.

"My Father...is greater than all," said Jesus, **"no one can snatch them out of my Father's hand" (John 10:29).** Jesus is our Friend and our Brother; He only wants to bring us to His Father who is **"greater than all,"** to this awesome Creator-Father who holds everything in His hand—past, present, and future. Jesus wants to bring us close to the heart of His Father so you and I are finally able to experience the true foundation of basic trust and stand on the solid rock of His eternal Fatherhood. We will all get to see this Father. He is your Father as well! Jesus spoke of Him as **"my Father and your Father" (John 20:17),** and this is what He will be—your Father and my Father.

You will have your very own personal experiences with your Father. The basic character of our eternal Father never changes. Yet, He will reveal Himself to you in an especially unique way. He revealed Himself to Paul in a different manner than to Peter, John, or Timothy. That's the beauty in it! You have a personal Father in Him, as well as a personal Mother (He, the Father, chose to introduce Himself to you by way of a very personal Motherhood). You will call Him, "My Father! You are mine!"

Eternal Father

Eternal Father—the Father of Creation

Whenever we talk about this Father, our very personal experiences with Him must be taken into consideration. The writers of the gospels shared how they experienced God the Father through Jesus; He is the eternal Word, which is one facet of His character. God is the Father of creation—He did not just cause a big bang and get the process of multiplication going by feeding the right programs into it. He created the universe from His Father's heart—not only as a genius of a Creator, but as a Father. Viewing creation from the perspective of a Father, He does not want anything to perish. It is His universe, the creation of a Father God.

For this very reason, Jesus could say: **"Consider the ravens: They do not sow or reap, they have no storeroom or barn; yet God feeds them..."** And He said, **"Consider how the lilies grow. They do not labor or spin. Yet I tell you, not even Solomon in all his splendor was dressed like one of these"** **(Luke 12:24,27).** The Maker of creation is a Father. As a Father, He had your image in His heart all along. He caused you to be born into this world by two human beings giving part of their own lives—a seed and a womb.

But still it was the Creator Father who formed you, not some reproductive act initiated by man and woman. God is all-knowing, all-powerful; this is His creation. Yet we are capable of aborting, destroying, and rejecting life. Jesus had to die on the cross to restore all things and, once again, make true life possible. Now redemption is able to reach and transform all of creation. It can rejoice and cheer once more. The psalmists wrote, "Clap your hands, you trees of the forest! You islands, rejoice! You mountains, be glad! Thunder, you mighty thunders to the glory of the Lord, and you waters roar!" (see Psalm 98:7-8). Together with us, creation shall worship the glory of God.

A couple of years ago we were in Ephesus, visiting the ruins of the amphitheater which among other functions had served as a gathering place for the political leadership of the city. Standing on the top rows, we prayed as a group. We prophesied over this field of rubble, but at the same time used the rubble to symbolically represent the church, which has endured much and worked sacrificially to honor her God.

We proclaimed the first love once again over the debris of the church, the body of Christ, who we envisioned there, scattered on the floor. Beautifully cut pieces of masonry with painted ornaments and symbols still on them could be found all over the place. We prophetically spoke to these pieces to gather again, to reform the glorious body of Christ. As we spoke the "amen" from the same elevated place where we were standing, we could hear a little bird singing its tune over those ruins. It sounded like God wanted to show us that His creation senses the coming day of redemption through the jubilant song of a bird who somehow knew: My Father who is nourishing me, the eternal Father in Jesus Christ, will come again into this world.

The Father's Heart Is Turned Toward Those Who Are Weak

It is beautiful to know that our Father's heart is especially moved by the weak. If we go over the healing accounts of Jesus, we notice that most of those who were being healed, with a few exceptions like the daughter of Jairus or the blind Bartimaeus, were nameless people, people who in many cases were just oozing with frailty and misery. They were battered not only with deafness, but often they were even speechless and dumb, born blind or lame, like the one saying, **"Sir... I have no one to help me into the pool when the water is stirred..." (John 5:7).**

Or think of the woman with the issue of blood, the poor thing—all of her money was gone when Jesus finally led her to the Father and restored her dignity. She left, no longer bent under her shame and in need to cover up her disease, but upright as an honorable woman, a daughter of Abraham, and a daughter of her eternal Father, a woman who had found security, basic trust, and a new self-esteem (see Mark 5:25-34).

Jesus said once: **"See that you do not look down on one of these little ones."** You may think, "How insignificant! This is totally pointless," but Jesus says, **"For I tell you that their angels in heaven always see the face of My Father in heaven" (Matthew 18:10).** Unimpressive people—these anonymous, average Joes and Janes—have angels who always see the face of the Father. Not every angel is granted this favorable position, many of them are just standing around the throne in a wide circle, but the angels of those weak ones have special access to the Father's throne. What a Father's heart!

He is our Creator Father who does not want anyone to be lost. Some people who are handicapped have a special glow on their faces, like a reflection of their eternal Father brought into their lives by an angel. Sometimes it can be seen in the smile of a dying person, suddenly lighting up the face. Could it be that after all the struggles for life are over and the person finally relaxes, the countenance is allowed to radiate? How can we explain this phenomenon? It is the eternal Father, the awesome Father of our Lord Jesus Christ, saying, "Welcome, My son!

Father

Welcome, My daughter! The struggle is over. You are in your Father's house right now because you were born again to a new life through the stripes of Jesus Christ!"

Think of the role the widows played in the gospels. Jesus was standing in the temple, watching people bringing their gifts to the treasury. Out of all those who deposited their offering, it was a poor widow who stood out to Him. Jesus called His disciples together and used her as an illustration to make a very important point: "You disciples, look at this woman! She is a true heroine in My kingdom, a real daughter of the eternal Father! She gave her eternal Father everything she owned—two small coins!" (see Mark 12:43,44). Or think of the story taking place in Nain (see Luke 7:11-17), where Jesus was deeply moved when He saw the only son of a widow being carried out of the village for burial. Jesus stopped and raised her son from the dead. This is the heart of a Father!

Think of the parable of the Good Samaritan, the story of the Samaritan woman at the well (see John 4:7-30), or the instance where noisy children were interrupting Jesus in His teaching. The mothers were rebuked and chased away by His disciples, but Jesus intervened, saying, **"Let the little children come to me!" (Mark 10:14)**, and He took them in His arms and blessed them.

How I Personally Experienced the Father

Let me share with you briefly how I experienced "my Father." I got to know Him as a Father who is patient, searching for me over and over again, never letting me down, in spite of my mistakes and failures. Jesus once said, **"...the Father judges no one, but has entrusted all judgment to the Son" (John 5:22)**.

Eternal Father

Unless you have given your life to Jesus here on earth, you will not stand before the Father on judgment day, but before Jesus Christ, the judge of the earth. The Father has handed over judgment to the Son and the day is coming when He will say, "All of the blessed ones of the Father, move over to this side! All those who are still under the curse move over to the other side!" (see Matthew 25:31-46).

It will not be the eternal Father who will be the Judge, but the Lamb of God, the eternal Son of God, who bears the marks of the cross on His body, who gave His life for you and for me, and who submitted Himself to the Father. He will be the One standing in front of you to pronounce judgment, not the Father.

The Father will be the Judge in the rewarding process. In other words, it is His privilege to pass out the rewards to His children. It is a special joy that He has reserved for Himself. It will be a glorious occasion, and I can hardly wait for this moment to come. Some Christians just have too rigid a picture of God to even imagine that we could really receive a reward in heaven. Besides, we are good Protestants who do not work for rewards, but who are saved by grace alone. But God is sovereign, and if He chooses to be generous, it is none of our business.

On that day, God will take His time to pass out the rewards and we will be totally overwhelmed and astounded. There will be rejoicing, no more envy, jealousy, and competition. There will only be joy and jubilation about our eternal Father who is loving and gracious beyond description! We will see people who never made a name for themselves, who are not mentioned in any history book—they might never even have entered a church. Yet they will be called to the throne on that day and they will hear the Father say, "This is for you, My child!"

Father

The angels in the band will blow their fanfare and all of us, millions upon millions, will join in the cheering and rejoice in our eternal Father as He passes out His rewards. Even though there will not be any need for gifts in eternity because we will already have everything, He will still enjoy spoiling us! Our God is the God of abundance and of riches. He always wanted to bless us, but during our lifetime we just were not bold enough to ask. Once we allow Him to finally give to us what He always intended, nothing will stop Him anymore.

This is how I have experienced my heavenly Father over and over again. So many times I was scared to death, convinced that I had messed up for good and there would not be any way out. But the Lord has always reached out to me. The book of Isaiah says, **"All day long I have held out my hands to an obstinate people, who walk in ways not good, pursuing their own imaginations" (Isaiah 65:2).** In the same way, the Lord always searched for me. I cannot think of anyone who would be as encouraging and as thoughtful as He is, anyone who knows about my heart and the things that make me happy like the Father does. He is aware of my most intimate secrets and He understands my needs.

I recall one particular area in which I struggled most in dealing with God as my Father. I really had to struggle with legalism over extended periods of my Christian life. Thus, in addition to my real sins which caused a lot of pain in my life, I was suffering from feelings of false guilt. Back then I had no idea how to break free from these issues. There were no "sin bins" like we use them today during some conferences, where people can dispose of their sins and receive forgiveness.

Eternal Father

Confession of sins in a one-on-one setting was not yet a widely accepted practice within the reformed, evangelical church back then. It was considered to be more or less a sectarian custom. Over and over again I had this condemnation come over me and I thought, "This time He's going to punish me real bad!" Then I would look down and let my shoulders droop. Those who knew me were aware that I had been dealing with my bodily posture for a long time. This habit goes back to a time when I would automatically take that posture in the presence of my dad, thinking "Now he's going to come after me again! If I look devout and submissive enough, he might still have mercy on me..."

I had to slowly learn that my heavenly Father is not punishing me, but that He has to discipline me. The punishment—in the sense of a penance, where I have to pay for things I have done wrong—fell on Jesus: **"The punishment that brought us peace was upon him" (Isaiah 53:5)**. I had to learn this distinction and come to an understanding that I have a Father who does not punish me, but nevertheless has to discipline me. He wants to help me become a man. Every father wants a real son who is able to take responsibility, a son representing him well, a son to be proud of. He wants to give him everything he has and show him everything he knows. In the same way, God is putting challenges before us. I used to get confused and misunderstand this concept. Today, I am thankful when I see challenges come my way.

Every spiritual leader or pastor is familiar with this. There are times when everything goes smoothly. You open your Bible and a passage is standing out to you. Before you know it, your sermon is halfway finished. In everything you do, there seems to be a spiritual flow. After you are done, you are looking forward to the next sermon because you have all these new ideas on your mind. But then there are times when you are going through a desert. You are flipping through your Bible and see all the highlighted Scriptures that remind you of the days when messages came to you easily and all you needed to do was just write down the things which flowed out of you.

Since then I have learned that I do not have to go on a guilt trip and blame myself for these times. I no longer assume that God must be punishing me for something. He just wants to teach me and lead me to a new place in Him. I just tell Him: "Thank You, Lord. This is a drag, but it's also exciting and I am fine with it! Let's go through this new training season together!" You are sweating and asking yourself how everything will work out, but again you let Him know: "Father, I am confident that we will make it together. Together we will scale this wall!"

Nothing Can Separate Us From His Love

As far as it is possible for a human being living in this world, we will eventually get to a point where we have an assurance which enables us to agree with Paul: "I am convinced that nothing will be able to separate us from the love of God" (see Romans 8:38-39). Do we believe we can actually reach a place of knowing, beyond any doubt that the Father will not punish or destroy us, nor will He take things away from us in order to rob us, but that He will instead discipline us to build us up as His sons or daughters, so our lives will honor His glory?

Jesus Himself learned this lesson. When Peter drew his sword in the Garden of Gethsemane, Jesus rebuked him and said, **"Put your sword back in its place ... Do you think I cannot call on my Father, and He will at once put at my disposal more than**

twelve legions of angels?" (Matthew 26:52-53). Twelve legions would be a total of 72,000 angels. Just take a few moments to imagine how the handful of Roman soldiers and servants of the High Priest would have been shocked if suddenly 72,000 angels with flaming swords had invaded the Garden of Gethsemane. They had already fallen to the ground when Jesus said, "It's me!" What if there had been 72,000 angels with Him?

Jesus knew for sure that nothing could separate Him from His Father and His love. He could have said to His Father at any minute: "Father, I need these angels." But He did not because He knew that "the Scriptures need to be fulfilled" (see Matthew 26:54), and He was aware that "nothing, nothing could ever separate Me from My Father's love! He will stay My Father! Even if I am made to be the sin of the world and go through the hell of division from God. Even if the pains of all kinds of sicknesses are going through Me a million fold, and the suffering of the world hits Me like electric shocks—all murder, manslaughter, torture, and hate that ever was and ever will be on the face of the earth!" All of this was heaped on Jesus at that very moment—on His Spirit, Soul, and Body. In His utter desperation, Jesus exclaimed, **"My God, my God, why have you forsaken me?" (Matthew 27:46),** praying a verse from Psalm 22, in order to fulfill the Scripture. Nonetheless, Jesus knew in His heart that nothing could ever separate Him from the love of God.

The better we get to know God, the closer we come to a point where we understand that "nothing whatsoever will be able to separate us from the love of God that is in Christ Jesus our Lord" (see Romans 8:38-39).

Father

There was yet another point where I had difficulties with God. He just did not seem to match my Christian view of how things are; He did not fit into my theology. It took me a long time to grasp that God does not fit into any theology. He just does not care about our human ideas of how God should behave—not even in services! God seems to have His own etiquette manual and it really gave me a hard time. If He had not put an angel by my side to help me get an understanding of who He is, I probably would have withdrawn over and over again. Slowly I started to realize that God is life, He is creative, and He does not fit into any box we try to force Him into. He will not be detained in any theological cages. Whenever we think we have a hold of Him, He will always burst the door open and do whatever is pleasing to Him. You cannot restrain God, but He sovereignly chose to reveal Himself in Jesus.

God Is a Mystery

Ultimately, God is a mystery. That always strikes me. There is this enigma about Him that just causes me to fall on my knees and worship His holiness. I know there is an endless universe of mysteries about this Father God that I am not even aware of. Maybe in eternity God will start revealing some of His secrets to us. Not even Jesus knew all of His Father's secrets! He said, **"No one knows about that day or hour, not even the angels in heaven, nor the Son, but only the Father" (Mark 13:32).** He is a God full of mysteries. You just have to fall on your knees like Paul, saying, **"Oh, the depth of the riches of the wisdom and knowledge of God! How unsearchable His judgments, and his paths beyond tracing out!" (Romans 11:33).** What an awesome God and Father we have! To worship means falling prostrate before Him to adore the mystery of His being, uttering,

Eternal Father

"Thank You Lord for revealing Yourself to me. Thank You for disclosing Your heart to me and enabling me to take off my shoes and stand in Your presence to behold Your mystery. For You are holy, holy, holy; kadosh, kadosh, kadosh—the 'I Am Who I Am.'"

What an awesome experience it will be to encounter the great mystery of our God face-to-face! We will no longer see Him through the Word of the Bible and through the person of Christ, His Son, but we will see Him in all of His fullness—the fullness of life. It will be the first time for us to see life for what it really is, as we will meet the true Source of it all! We will hear the four living creatures around the throne speaking with voices of thunder (see Revelation 6:1). Lightning and voices will go out from the throne of God. Like the prophets, we will see the fiery wagon of God.

What will it be like to stand before the mystery of God, the eternal Father who is the Creator of everything? He created His own Son to become our Friend and Brother, that He might lead us back to the Father's heart, back to the awesome, eternal Father. What will it be like to finally sense and experience real life? I am not talking about life here on earth which is still marked by death, having to stand its ground against the forces of destruction like a smoldering wick, with a fearful, trembling heart or with a scream of desperation. I am talking about pure life and pure love, the burning furnace of God that Luther described.

You and I will be standing before God, the eternal Father as His very sons and daughters, transformed into the image of Jesus Christ. We will worship Him! Is it not marvelous that Jesus taught us the Father's prayer? **"Our Father!..." (Matthew 6:9)** In his translation of the Bible, Luther even reversed it to "Father of ours." "Father of ours!" "Father of ours!" We could say it a million times: "Father of ours!" I don't know how often I have said it, and yet I am not aware of one single time that I just said it mechanically. It is simply unfathomable, like the Father Himself is unfathomable.

Revival Means Drawing Close to the Father

I am convinced that revival means nothing else other than to be released to draw close to the Father, so our spirit and soul can be satisfied and we can come to the very foundation of our Father's love for us. Then nothing will be able to overcome us—nothing! **"If we live, we live to the Lord; and if we die, we die to the Lord. So, whether we live or die, we belong to the Lord" (Romans 14:8).** Revival will bring to us once again a revelation of the Father's goodness and love. It has started already in many parts of the world. Multitudes are getting to know the Father, prompting the angels to rejoice over the sinner who repents because he has discovered who God is. Nothing could ever hinder Him from holding His precious child close to His heart again.

FIVE

The Father's Approval
The Very Foundation of Our Lives

"**D**o not let your hearts be troubled. Trust in God; trust also in Me.

In my Father's house are many rooms; if it were not so, I would have told you. I am going there to prepare a place for you.

And if I go and prepare a place for you, I will come back and take you to be with me that you also may be where I am.

You know the way to the place where I am going." Thomas said to Him, "Lord, we don't know where

You are going, so how can we know the way?"

Jesus answered, "I am the way and the truth and the life. No one comes to the Father except through Me.

If you really knew Me, you would know My Father as well. From now on, you do know him and have seen him."

Philip said, "Lord, show us the Father and that will be enough for us."

Jesus answered: "Don't you know me, Philip, even after I have been among you such a long time? Anyone who has seen me has seen the Father. How can you say, 'Show us the Father?'

"Don't you believe that I am in the Father, and that the Father is in me? The words I say to you are not just My own. Rather, it is the Father, living in me, who is doing His work.

Believe me when I say that I am in the Father and the Father is in me; or at least believe on the evidence of the miracles themselves.

I tell you the truth, anyone who has faith in me will do what I have been doing. He will do even greater things than these, because I am going to the Father.

And I will do whatever you ask in my name, so that the Son may bring glory to the Father. You may ask Me for anything in My name, and I will do it" (John 14:1-14).

The Fundamental Question of Mankind

It is amazing how the deepest truth can be expressed in a simple question. Philip and Thomas did not even realize how their inept questions contained a profound reality. When Philip asked, **"Lord, show us the Father and that will be enough for us,"** he raised one of the fundamental questions of mankind. We have to know the Father and when we do, this is all we need. Only then are we standing on solid ground, on a secure foundation that can never be shaken.

And this is the reason why: We need the affirmation of the Father in order to live and feel safe. Creation is designed to begin small like a seed, like the pistil of a flower being pollinated, like an egg cell being fertilized. It begins tiny, invisibly in a shell, or in the depths of a mother's womb until it pushes through the cervix or breaks through the shell restraining it, straining towards the light. Life starts out small, insignificant, hidden, unacknowledged, and without form, like the prophet Isaiah said, **"He has no form or comeliness..." (Isaiah 53:2 NKJV).**

The Creator's Approval

Every living being is insignificant and unimpressive at the outset; this is true for all creation. Creation is never instant. Nothing begins impressively; every living being is unassuming, lowly, and hidden until it matures and breaks through to become visible. Because this is reality and everything within us also has to go through this stage of lowliness and concealment, we are desperately waiting for the word of approval: "You are good! Approved! You may go your way and live! Reproduce and multiply! Take your place! It is well with you!"

We can find this illustrated in creation. One day, I was taking a walk in a meadow and decided to look closely at a small blade of grass. While I was kneeling there, scrutinizing it, the Lord spoke to me about the nobility of His creation. This was just an ordinary blade of grass. It did not have any sophisticated features; it did not have a beautiful flower attached to it. There was nothing special about it. No surprises like the marvelous blossom of the Queen of the Night that blooms a single night only—just an ordinary, unassuming blade of grass. Yet, there was such poise emanating from that humble creature.

Have you ever noticed that? It has nothing to show forth to make itself more respectable. It is just what it is—ordinary grass, swayed by the wind, bent and trampled on, lifting itself up again. It has the approval of its Creator built into it. Thus it can exist with a divine sense of dignity. It may be overshadowed by the disapproval of men that we impose on certain species of creation saying, "This is just a weed, just a tick, just a gnat. It is good for nothing." And yet the divine approval is once and for all built into these creatures. They are carrying an unshakable sense of affirmation because their Creator once looked at them and **"saw that it was good" (Genesis 1:12).**

Just imagine the dignity of a lion or even an ordinary house cat. Have you ever watched a cat settling down, stretching itself lazily? It would require a lot of physical therapy on our end to attain such a graceful bearing! Just imagine the pose of a cat stretching out on a lawn chair, deeply relaxed and yet full of elegance, one paw resting on top of the other, her eyelids blinking in the sun and her head just slightly bent to the side, as if she had practiced her posture in front of a mirror. You can tell that she is secure in the divine approval that her Maker once expressed over her; you can still hear her purring: "It is marvelous. It is good!"

What do you think is driving the birds to trill away at sunrise before they have even had breakfast? It is the divine approval of their Creator. These little creatures are reflecting back something that was deposited in them. Is there anything more beautiful than the jubilant song of a lark or it spreading out its wings, soaring up from its nest?

The approval of the Creator is still resonating deep within every living thing and yet, at the same time, there is a moaning and groaning in every creature because somehow creation is aware that man, the very image of God, has been crushed by divine disapproval. As a consequence, all mankind carries a basic sense of disapproval instead of the approval of God. We were appointed to rule over creation, but we keep poisoning it instead with the venom which has infested our hearts.

We are in desperate need of divine approval. Adam, the first man, had this kind of assurance. For this reason he could stand naked before God. We have no need to cover things up once we have this divine affirmation on our life. There is no need to prove ourselves before God or in the eyes of creation. After all, it was God the Creator and Father Himself who proclaimed over us, "Wonderful! You were made in My likeness! You are fully approved!" Only this affirmation releases man to be!

Broken Fatherhood and Motherhood

All fatherhood and motherhood which is no longer fueled and invigorated by the living Source is subject to distortion. It is only a shadow of what it could be. I do not mean to put condemnation on anybody; it is just a matter of fact that we need the reconciliation of the cross in order to be able to fulfill the roles of a father and mother. Yes, there are people who are especially skillful in their roles as parents. There are even those who may be called an ideal father or mother. Most people are looking forward to the birth of their child from the depths of their hearts. And yet over the generations there has been something lurking at the bottom of our human nature, a sense of suspicion, a knowing that we are only humans. As hard as we may try to become perfect parents, our children will always know whether our approval is true and genuine.

Children keep asking, "Do you love me? Do you really love me?" Even when they are grown up and married, they may still fish for the affirmation of a father or mother. What is the driving force behind such behavior patterns? It is the lack of trust that is deeply rooted in us. Over and over we ask the same questions: "Is the affirmation of our parents really honest? Does it apply even if I am totally out of it for a time? Is it irrevocable and definite or is it conditional? Am I still approved as a person if I failed the college entrance exam? Does it apply if I come home with a baby and do not even know who the father is? Am I really approved once and for all?"

God never takes back His approval. He is truth and He cannot lie. The Bible teaches, **"God is not a man, that he should lie..." (Numbers 23:19).** When God says "yes" to us, that is exactly what He means. He says, "I have made a covenant with you and I swear that I will keep it." This covenant was sealed with the blood of His Son. If God approves us, this approval will last for all eternity. Our spirit is somehow aware of this. Therefore, Philip could make this amazing statement, **"Lord, show us the Father and that will be enough for us."** Show us the Father, who in Himself is the Truth. I need to hear it from Him personally: "Yes, you are My daughter and My son! You are approved and you shall live! Take your place! Now run the race and feel the wind on your face!"

There are strong fathers whom we can look up to. Daughters adore them and sons can measure their strength on them. But we also know about the dangers of such a strong father figure. His shadow will be over them wherever they go. As hard as they may try, they cannot break free from his influence. Besides, there may be these hidden expectations that sometime in the future they will take over the farm or the family business. A father may try to impose on his son some of the goals he himself could not reach. And, of course, there are weak fathers of whom we are ashamed. It feels as though they are of no help to us because they are unable to show us how to live our lives. If this is our experience, it may seem like a burden we are bearing that distorts something deep inside of us. Sometimes we may even have to fight feelings of contempt.

Christian Homes

If we have grown up in a Christian home, things can sometimes become really complicated. Inevitably we start mixing up the images that are being conveyed to us by earthly fathers and mothers with our image of God. We try so hard to be the good Christian children that everybody in church expects us to be. So much pain is being concealed behind the nice facades of Christian homes! There are parents who pray over their kids day and night, manipulating them with their tears and prayers and expectations. They are trying so hard to point them in the right direction and to shield them from the harmful influences of the world that they may even read their diaries secretly to detect and wrestle down any hint of evil. I am talking about Christian parents!

It is time for us to admit that we as fathers and mothers are oftentimes misrepresenting our heavenly Father. Our ability to be fathers and mothers to our children is a gift of the Holy Spirit and it is important for us to release our children into the hands of God. We must release them to go their own ways. We must be willing to give them their share of the estate, their share of privacy, and room enough for their own experiences. We must stop coddling them, removing every obstacle from their paths.

How many pastors' homes have become like launching pads into a godless lifestyle? Vicious intellectuals, cynics, harsh critics of the faith have been raised in pastors' homes. But God says, "Leave it to Me! You need not be the perfect Christian father. You need not be a flawless Christian mother. Your children do not need to be picture-perfect Christian kids. I am the God who made them and they need to hear My approval, not your patronizing, anxious, and pushy acceptance, which only amounts to mere manipulation." What your children need is divine affirmation by their heavenly Father, who is the Truth.

The Father's Approval of Jesus

God expressed His approval of His Son, Jesus Christ. I am convinced that Mary had a very positive attitude toward the child she was bearing and was filled with joyful expectancy during her pregnancy. If there was ever a mother who felt a deep sense of acceptance for her child, it was Mary. And yet God knew that even the heartfelt approval of a mother was not enough. God Himself opened the heavens, angels sang, a star rose above the stable, and shepherds and kings came, bowing their knees, bringing gifts of gold, myrrh, and frankincense. Only a short time later, there were old Simeon and Hannah, the prophetess, testifying in the temple to the divine approval of Jesus, on the day that Mary and Joseph came to offer their poor man's sacrifice of two doves for their Son.

God took His time to deeply implement His Fatherly approval into His Son during His thirty years of preparation in Nazareth. At His baptism, just before Jesus' story of public rejection began, He opened the heavens once again above the Jordan River and made His voice heard, the voice of the Creator and Father: **"This is My Son, whom I love; with him I am well pleased"** **(Matthew 3:17).**

The Father's Approval

On the mount of transfiguration, the heavens opened for a third time and God affirmed His Son once again, by pouring out the glory of the Creator God over Him (see Matthew 17:1-13). Jesus radiated, His face became like the sun, and His garments were white as snow. He talked to Moses and Elijah, just before the cloud hid them, leaving Him alone with the three disciples. After this experience, He descended to heal the demon-possessed boy, before He moved directly up to Jerusalem. From then on, the heavens would remain locked up, like brass. But the earth quaked and rocks burst, as the Son of God cried out, "'Eloi, Eloi, lama sabachthani?'—which means, **'My God, my God, why have you forsaken me?'"** (Matthew 27:46).

The approval of the Father shaped the life of Jesus; it marked Him and His walk on earth in the power of the Holy Spirit. With this approval on His life, He visited the houses of tax collectors and sinners. With this approval, He could allow a prostitute to wash His feet with her tears and to dry them with her hair, while Pharisees and scribes were watching with disgust (see Luke 7:37-39). With this approval on His life, He fulfilled the tasks assigned to Him by the Father with these creative acts of the Creator God.

With this approval on His life, He stood before Pilate saying, "You are right, I am a King. I was born and came into the world to testify to the truth" (see John 18:37). I came to proclaim divine approval over broken mankind, over these belittled and broken creatures, over people whose lives are under the shadows of fathers, mothers, and authority figures with their lofty expectations. He came to proclaim the Creator's approval over them, once again!

For this reason, there is **"Yes"** and **"Amen"** in Jesus to all the promises of God (see II Corinthians 1:20). Through His blood, the new and eternal covenant was established for all mankind. A new mankind was proclaimed with Jesus being the first new man, the last Adam, (see II Corinthians 15:45) the firstborn of many brothers and sisters (see Romans 8:29).

SIX

Jesus
The Image of the Father

J esus said, "No one comes to the Father except through Me. If you really knew Me, you would know My Father as well. From now on, you do know Him and have seen Him" (John 14:6). A little later, He said to Philip, "Anyone who has seen Me has seen the Father. How can you say, 'Show us the Father?'" (John 14:9)

The Father that Jesus was talking about in these verses can only be recognized in Him. This Father is not just a projection of our deep longing for love and approval. We may paint delightful pictures of a loving father, the way we always dreamed a father to be. Our soul loves to expand on dreams of what a true father should be like. But these are just images of something we once knew and they still echo deep within us. And yet this is not reality.

The "Father of all Fatherhood" exceeds by far, all of those inner images and yearnings of our soul. By far! The Father knows your innermost being. He loves you. But not just that, He honors you. He honors you. Are you aware of what that means? To love someone is a beautiful thing, but to honor is still somewhat different. He is a Father who does not belittle His children. Everything He has, He gives to His sons and daughters. Only the best is good enough for them—His Son, His own heart, the gifts of His Spirit and fellowship with Him, the Creator and Father. He feels drawn to us. He wants to be around us. He washes our feet. Words cannot express the depth of the Father's love for us. It far exceeds the dreams of our yearning hearts.

Slamming the Door in View of His Grace

If you start preaching the gospel of His love, people start slamming doors, running off scandalized and full of anger. You can find this throughout the Bible. As soon as the Father appears, you will hear slamming doors because we cannot imagine God to be so full of compassion and love. It just does not compute with us. He is so compassionate toward the lost that we tend to take offense in it. We find it unbalanced, extreme, and unwarranted!

All through the Old Testament slamming doors could be heard, and of course, this pattern did not change when Jesus came. When the prodigal son came home, the father spontaneously launched a huge welcome party. Only the best was good enough (see Luke 15:22-24). Would not a little goat have done it as well? He could have added some tasty gravy with a lot of thyme and marjoram to cover up the "goaty" taste. God, however, takes His best.

The fattened calf, which was supposed to be a special treat for the whole family, was just right. And not just that, but in broad daylight when people are supposed to be working, he drummed up the musicians and gave everybody a day off to come over and celebrate and dance with him. But suddenly you heard the familiar sound of doors being slammed. The older brother, who had stayed with the father all along and who should know him well, came home from work. He was furious: "How can you do this? I'm not going in there!" (see Luke 15:28). The same scene can be witnessed all the time, wherever the real gospel is being proclaimed. The gospel is good news! But we would rather prefer news that, well, has some good to it, but that is still sensible. The gospel is good news, not a morally tinted, well-balanced, decent message. It is breaking news, groundbreaking news. That is why we see people slamming their door right in God's face, even to this day.

Martin Luther's Breakthrough

Let us think of Martin Luther for a moment. This man had tremendous courage! He dug out the good news, at first for himself personally. He had tried to buy the Father's love with an austere lifestyle, until suddenly when he was reading the Word he had his famous "tower experience." God took him up on a tower and revealed to him what the gospel was all about. God proclaimed His approval over this beer-bellied man, who enjoyed coarse jokes, had so many rough edges and a heart full of scars and wrinkles. Yet there was a deep desperate cry in his soul, like the deer panting for the water brooks. God proclaimed He loved him, "just the way you are, Doc Martin."

After Martin Luther received the divine approval, he penned it in the form of his 95 theses and nailed it to the door of a church in Wittenberg. Later on, he started preaching the divine approval, but that was not all. Because he knew that his message was not just the opinion of a church reformer, but came from God Himself, he started translating the Word of God, which contained the good news, into a language the ordinary people could understand. The Word itself is the good news. It is the gospel. Whoever reads and absorbs His Word becomes saturated with divine approval and with God's truth. Like Martin Luther, he will find himself standing on that tower, hearing God speak to his heart: "Start looking into the distance! Your life can start all over again."

The New Man

God just does not match with our preconceived ideas. He is full of mercy and compassion. He carried all of our sins to the cross of Golgotha. All of them! He paid the price to the last penny! Everything has been paid for! There is no debt remaining! Jesus did not abolish God's law; He fulfilled it completely. Then He said, "I have come to inhabit you and I will write My law into your heart. I will do that by depositing My love into your heart. 'I in you' will be the strength to be and to live as a new person."

Some people like to think of themselves as "adopted" sons and daughters of God. I have serious problems with this "theology of adoption." In my opinion, it is bad theology. We can only think of ourselves as being adopted by God if we have not really understood the good news. As an adopted child, I am some kind of "son on paper" or "daughter on paper." God did not adopt us; He begot us. He is our true Father. John made it quite clear when he said that we **"were born, not of blood nor of the will of the flesh nor of the will of man, but of God"** (John 1:13 NAS).

The Creator God begot us—you and me, through the Holy Spirit and through the blood of Christ. We are a new creation.

Jesus

We are not talking about a little refurbishing of the old man: God begot you anew when you were born again. Can you imagine what that means? When Paul spoke of a **"new creation"** in II Corinthians 5:17, he was not referring to a major overhaul of something old, like a second-hand car that was being waxed and polished until it sparkled like new. I really do not know how these car dealerships do that. People turn in their old car and the next time you pass by, there it is, looking like a brand-new car. It looks almost better than your new car and you wonder why you even sold it.

God, however, creates something new in us. He begets you and me anew, by His Spirit and by the blood of His Son. Through this divine act of creation, the inner man is being formed in us. In the beginning, our new man is rather unappealing and people at home may say things like, "You—a Christian? Don't give me that! You're just plain, old you like always!"

Oftentimes things really do not look much different from what they used to be. For this reason, you need to dig into the Word of God. If you do not make an effort to clothe yourself with the truth every morning, you will certainly get confused. You will always question yourself: "Am I a total failure? I should be a witness of Christ to my family and to the people in church, proving to them that I really am a new creation!" That is nonsense! You do not need to prove anything, but you must feed yourself on the truth in order for this new creation, the inner man that God created in you to grow. Do you think Moses became the most humble person on earth overnight? He used to be a violent murderer! Do you think change came easily to a staunch Pharisee and legalistic perfectionist like Paul?

Father

No More X-rays

You need not continually x-ray your inner man. My dentist always makes it appear really harmless when he says, "Well, let's take a little picture." A "little picture," however, means that my body will be exposed to another load of x-rays. The same applies to our spiritual life. Those "little pictures" are radioactive and dangerous. Leave it up to God to convict you! God is the One who created the new man in you and He proclaimed His divine approval over you: "It is good!" Every morning, as you get up, pick up your Bible and clothe yourself with the truth. You will get to hear it over and over: "Very well, My daughter! Very well, My son! Everything is fine; just hold on. Together we will scale the walls today." There is no more condemnation because He is a true Father!

You see, the problem is that people always want to be punished or, at the very least, they want to be disapproved. People would prefer God's love to be just a little more conditional. Unfortunately, He will not do us this favor. What did Jesus do when He appeared to the disciples after His resurrection? (see John 20:19-23) He said, "Peace! Shalom!" and showed them His wounds. His intention was not to make them feel miserable so they would finally understand how pitiful they really were. He showed them His wounds in order to demonstrate: "I have risen. I have come to proclaim the approval of the Father once again over you!"

These men were cowards—pathetic people who could not even stay awake with Him for one hour. Had they not been nourished by their Master's faith for three years? Were they not the eyewitnesses of everything He had done in the name of the Father—things like walking on water in the middle of the night while they struggled with the wind and the waves? What a wonderful friend! And yet they turned their backs on Him in His darkest hour. Now He returned to them proclaiming, **"Peace be with you!" (Verses 19 and 21).** He even breathed on them, giving them authority to forgive sins: **"If you forgive anyone his sins, they are forgiven…" (Verse 23).** At the same time, He commissioned them: **"As the Father has sent me, I am sending you" (Verse 21).**

They walked away embarrassed. Peter and his gang went back to the Sea of Tiberias to fish. After a very unsuccessful night of fishing, Jesus appeared on the shore and called out to them: **"Friends, haven't you any fish?" (John 21:5).** That is our God in His mercy and love!

If you messed up really good and are laying there, flat on your face, broken and ashamed, He comes and says to you, "Friend, haven't you anything to eat? Let Me wash you and lift you up. Stand up on your feet and throw out the net once again!" Because of His love, we are able to confess our sins, redress ourselves, and follow the Father who approves us. That is how His mercy and compassion works. No longer will we yield to those lying and disapproving voices.

No Condemnation

"Therefore, there is now no condemnation for those who are in Christ Jesus" (Romans 8:1). None at all! We confess our sins because we are overwhelmed by the love and compassion of our Father. We want His love to fill us and to touch every single cell of our body. It is our desire to have everything removed from us that is contrary to His love. We are overcome by the mercy of God.

We need the truth, this **"belt of truth,"** to be buckled around our waist (see Ephesians 6:14). You cannot live without it. When Paul described the armor of God, the **"belt of truth"** was the first component to be mentioned. We are tempted to lie as long as we have breath within us. You may be a "father in Christ," a "mother of Israel," or an anointed apostle, yet you are no exception. Many have fallen prey to lies. There is only one protection: We need to put on the **"belt of truth"** first thing every morning.

I myself have been practicing this for a long time. Every morning I proclaim: "Thank You, Father, that I am Your son. I am made righteous by faith! Thank You, Father, You have chosen me. You have ordained me to be transformed into the image of Your Son. You have called me with Your holy call and have given me Your righteousness, the righteousness of Your Son. You have sanctified me in Your truth and allowed me to share in Your glory. You have given me sisters and brothers and friends and You have become my friend Yourself."

Sometimes I take the **"belt of truth"** and punch a few more "holes" into it. A few favorite phrases are not enough; we need to add new "holes" every once in a while. God will keep showing you new aspects of His truth, and you will punch a new hole into the belt each time so the buckle can be attached to this new spot as well. The **"belt of truth"** is the belt of divine approval on your life. "Go! Walk! Take your place! Accept your dignity as My daughter, as My son!"

Casting Off the "If Onlys"

Many are still hurting from experiences they had growing up in Christian homes. There are also many mothers and fathers still condemning themselves for the way they brought up their children. They wish they could undo some of the mistakes they made raising their children or make up for some of the things they did not do: "If only I had been a better father…!" "If only I had not done this and that as a mother…!" I personally believe it is a sin to roam in the past. We are guilty of unbelief if we hold on to our "if only's," because we are declaring that God is dependent on our ability to do everything right to accomplish what He wants to do in the lives of our children.

Our God is the One who created the whole universe out of nothing. He is very well able to create royal sons and daughters with the charm of divine dignity on their lives, even though our fathering and mothering may have been severely flawed. They may have to go through deep places of disgrace and shame, but in the end, they will love much because they have been forgiven much.

Think of the prostitute who poured perfume on Jesus' feet, kissing them, wetting them with her tears and drying them with her hair (see Luke 7:37-38). She was one of the few people who understood the Father's approval. It is valid amidst all of our brokenness, amidst the desperate cries of our soul, when we feel like we have reached the end of our rope and cry out, "This illegitimate pregnancy killed me. This abortion was the end of it. The fact that I neglected my children so badly, back when they needed me most, is just inexcusable; there will be no way to make up for it!"

Let me tell you dear brother or dear sister: This is a language of unbelief and it is dishonoring to God. You are entertaining idols in your life if you are holding onto your "if only's." Stop getting in God's way and surrender your regrets to Him. Smash your altars and all of your ideas of how you should have done things. Just come to God, admitting, "God, I did it wrong. Everything is messed up, but still I will smash the altar of shame, self-accusation, and self-condemnation, of unfulfilled dreams and of the many 'if only's.' Life is moving on, and I will also stand to my feet and move on!"

Think of David. When the fruit of his adulterous affair with Bathsheba was about to die, he cried out to God in despair, pleading with Him to spare the child. He put on sackcloth and slept on the floor, refusing to eat or drink. After the baby had died, nobody dared to give him the news. But when he finally realized his son was dead, he stood up, washed and perfumed himself, and went to eat and drink (see II Samuel 12:16-20). David pulled down the altar of the "if only!" Later, God gave David, whom He loved, another son out of his relationship with Bathsheba. This son, Solomon, was to become his successor and the wisest man in the entire Old Testament, and made Bathsheba an ancestor to Jesus, the Messiah.

God is using our failures, troubles, and the painful mistakes that leave us totally broken and discouraged to build His kingdom, advance His work, and bring forth fruit for eternity. Your appealing facade may be broken, but God uses what is left to guide you and me into our destiny. Sons and daughters may have been browbeaten by perfectionist, dominant fathers; young women may have been overlooked and neglected, but God will restore beauty and dignity to us and bring out the true glory of our lives.

Our shortcomings are the construction material God uses for the building of His kingdom. Do not stay at the gravesites of your earthly ideals of fatherhood and motherhood. God is telling you to stop weeping and mourning. He is calling you by your name and He adds: "Yes, you are the one I mean! I am writing your name with golden letters. You are called to do My works. You are called to spread your wings and to soar in the wind of My Holy Spirit. In My lovingkindness, I will test you, discipline you, teach you, and train you. I have a deep passion in Me to build you up and to reward you. I am longing to present you to My angels and to My Son, saying, 'There she is! My daughter! There he is! My son!'"

I pray that those who want to leave behind their old burdens would forgive their fathers and mothers. I pray that fathers and mothers who are living under a cloud of self-condemnation, of "if only's," would drop their shortcomings at the cross and rededicate their children to God. Place them in His hands and dedicate them to Him. Give them back to God so He can turn the hearts of sons and daughters back to their fathers. Let Him also turn your heart to your own father and mother, so you can once again bless them and thank them for everything they have done, as imperfect as it may have been, and also for the things that God blessed you with in the midst of all the brokenness.

The Father's Challenges

God is very different, not only in His love and compassion, but also in the challenges He puts before us. For this reason, Jesus said with regard to His Father: **"anyone who has faith in me will do what I have been doing. He will do even greater things than these..."** (John 14:12). What is the Father's passion, the object of His ambition? It is to see His Son increase! He wants to see Him even surpass Himself, if that is possible! He wants to see dignity, freedom, and power reflected in His Son. Is that not a father's desire for his sons and daughters? I want them to rise to the top of their potential! Do not get me wrong; I am not saying that I intend to push them to be successful at any cost, but I want to see them seize abundant life! I want to see them take the land of their lives. I want to see what God has placed inside them unfold.

That is what the heavenly Father longed to see in His Son. Even as a twelve-year-old, He astounded university professors in Jerusalem. God had trained Him up for that. His training ground was the carpenter's workshop, among glue pots and finicky customers, in petty-minded Nazareth. That was His boot camp. God trained His Son to become longsuffering and patient, humble and wise, to seek the heart of His heavenly Father, and to always stay close to Him, to live a hidden life, desiring nothing for Himself, being a misapprehended, rejected eccentric. That is where Jesus learned His lessons.

Later, God elevated His Son and gave Him the name above all names in heaven and on earth. He placed the judgment over all nations and all the peoples of the earth in His hands. Jesus will pronounce judgment over the earth. It is He who will break the seal of heaven and of the history of the world.

That is another facet of our heavenly Father. Once He pronounces His approval over us and makes us His disciples, our cozy lifestyles and comfort zones will be constantly challenged. We will not just sit in church, warming the pews. We will not spend our time on nice little responsibilities that we have somehow managed to get a hold of, clinging to them for the rest of our lives because we identify ourselves with them.

Our heavenly Father longs to train His sons and daughters through challenging circumstances, building them up to do His work, and by the power of His Holy Spirit to do even greater works than Jesus did. This is the Father's will for us. He does not want us to be pathetic sons. We may sing about the "worm in the dust," and Dr. Martin Luther said toward the end of his life, *"For sure, we are beggars!"* Yet, during his lifetime, he had turned the world upside down. God wants to deliver us out of inferiority and petty-mindedness; He wants us to embrace the great callings He placed upon our lives and to do His work.

Bringing Home Gold for the King

At the great Olympic ski-jump in Innsbruck are the bowls in which the Olympic fire burned. There are also bronze tablets bearing the names of the athletes who won Olympic medals. As humans, we tend to admire such inscriptions, but we fail to realize that our names are written in heaven—not just at some great Olympic ski-jump, but in heaven!

Are you aware of what that means? We are not talking about some pathetic little housekeeping books or bits of paper scattered all over the place where somebody keeps scribbling names on empty corners whenever a person comes to Christ. These names are being written in golden letters. It is our heavenly Father writing the names of His sons and daughters in gold and the angels and heavenly hosts are standing there in front of these tablets, gazing admiringly at our names. There is a swoosh of flapping wings in front of these tablets with the golden letters on them! Hallelujah! And they have your name written on them. Did you get that?

God is counting on you! You have an indispensable position in the kingdom of God! God has given you an important part to play. From the very beginning, He assigned you a task and made room for you in His kingdom. You are called to do the works of God. Whether they are small and insignificant in your own eyes, or big and weighty—they are the works God has prepared in advance for you. Is that not marvelous?

Father

However, we do need to be trained for our purposes. The Father can be very firm with us, and, often, He will go to the limit of what we are able to take, but the final result is worth it. If athletes who are training for the Olympics have to stretch themselves to the very limit, do you not think God would stretch our souls to the limit as well? There are many trials and challenges coming our way, but we should be willing to take them on because we are heading for a goal.

I know of a story that happened many years ago during an Olympic swimming contest. The eyes of the public were fixed on a German swimmer who was expected to win. Yet there was also a little lady from Costa Rica in this particular race that had been rigorously prepared to her limits by her coach. She brought a little flag and placed it furtively by the side of her starter-block because she wanted to wave the flag of her country if she happened to win. She won the gold medal!

How about us? Let us bring home gold for our King!

Prayer

Father, we want to thank You for Your precious approval. All too often we have not responded to You with the respect You deserved. Thank You for renewing Your approval that You formerly accorded to Your Jewish people, to the fathers Abraham, Isaac, and Jacob, to Moses in the desert at the burning bush, to a people of slaves, to Your people under King Saul and King David and under the prophets. We want to thank You Lord that Your approval took the form of flesh and blood in Your Son so we could touch and embrace it. It became tangible for us to taste and see and feel. Yet, in the end, we turned our backs on You and crucified Your Son because we could not handle the drastic display of Your love any longer.

Jesus

We slammed the door and have kept the mercy of the Father over His children away from us. But the Father raised You from the dead and since then You keep proclaiming the Father's approval to the world through Your Holy Spirit. You keep knocking at the doors of our hearts, asking, "May I place the approval of the Father into your heart? May I bless you again with this all-surpassing approval?"

I praise You, Father, over every one here, who was begotten by You, every new creation, everything that is maturing inside one of Your children, however concealed and unsightly it may be, and over everything that has already taken form, in open faces with beaming eyes, in a posture that expresses dignity. I praise You, Father, for the men and women and teenagers who are worshipfully doing the work of Your kingdom.

*Jesus, You said, **"No one knows the Father except the Son and those to whom the Son chooses to reveal Him"** (Matthew 11:27). So, we ask You to once again reveal to us the depth of the abundance of the Father. I plead with You Lord to help us discard at the foot of the cross the old broken images of what it means to be a father or a mother or to be under a father's or a mother's care. May You, Holy Spirit, place the new image of fatherhood and motherhood into our spirits and into our souls. I thank You for doing that Lord. Then we will be able to say like Philip: It is enough! I have found the ground where I can be anchored for all eternity. It is the stripes of Jesus, the heart of the Father, His mercy and His approval. It is steadfast and irrevocable, for the Jews, for the Gentiles, for everyone who seeks Him. Thank You Jesus.*

SEVEN

Sons and Daughters of the Father

A New Sense of Dignity

During His Sermon on the Mount, Jesus prayed, **"But I tell you: Love your enemies and pray for those who persecute you, that you may be sons of your Father in heaven. He causes his sun to rise on the evil and the good, and sends rain on the righteous and the unrighteous. If you love those who love you, what reward will you get? Are not even the tax collectors doing that? And if you greet only your brothers, what are you doing more than others? Do not even pagans do that? Be perfect, therefore, as your heavenly Father is perfect"** (Matthew 5:44-48).

This is the only passage in the New Testament that gives such an outright command to be perfect, as our Father in heaven is perfect. We have to be careful, however, not to understand this command in terms of immaculate faultlessness, or whatever we tend to imagine when we are confronted with claims of perfection.

The only perfect thing in the kingdom of God is the love of the Father. It is the love that **"sends rain on the righteous and**

the unrighteous" and causes the sun to rise on the good and the evil; this, and this alone, is true perfection. There is no other perfection. There are no perfect marriages, nor are there any perfect friendships. There are no perfect fellowships, nor are there any perfect churches. There are no perfect committees, ministries, movements, conferences, or worship services—Jesus never intended it to be that way. We are wasting our energy if we insist on doing things perfectly.

Perfect Love in All of Our Imperfection

This is especially true for our churches! Over and over we have hampered the advance of the kingdom by our attempts to create outstanding churches. We tend to forget that God has always meant churches to be limited, to be fragments which need to be complemented, places that portray only a facet of the rich diversity in God's kingdom. If we want to see the kingdom of God expand, we need to leave the obsession that we have to create something perfect behind us.

We also need to get beyond expectations that our relationships need to be perfect. Love can only grow and spread in earthly vessels; it cannot function otherwise. How can we forgive one another if everything is perfect? It is a wonderful experience when suddenly, in the midst of painful disagreements, we realize that we need to forgive one another and come to a point of mutual understanding. It is one of the most beautiful things in the kingdom of God to surrender our claims and admit that all of our churches, denominations, and movements are only parts of a much larger picture and thus are appropriately incomplete. They need to be complemented. The more we become aware of this, the more we start praying: "Lord, lead us into Your perfect love and help us to embrace each other in spite of our imperfections."

Sons and Daughters of the Father

However, if His perfect love enters into our imperfections, limitations, and shortcomings, we see a remarkable difference. A marriage relationship may still be as flawed and defective as it has always been, but when the Father's love enters, it brings wholeness. Your wife still may not be a fabulous housekeeper; your husband still may not be a handyman. He may stay as clumsy as ever, but if true love is restored, it causes things to be all right. The same is true for our churches. If the Father's love and compassion invades our hearts, things will be all right.

The Dignity of the Sons and Daughters of God

For this reason our text says, "**...that you may be sons of your Father in heaven.**" Jesus came into this world, proclaiming the news that God lives, that He is a Father, and that we are called to be His sons and daughters. Jesus gave us an example of what it means to be "a son of the Father." Jesus was a man like you and me, just like the Bible says about Elijah, "**Elijah was a man just like us**" **(James 5:17)**. This applies to every man in the Bible, even if he happens to have a pleasant name like Isaiah or Jeremiah. Even Jesus Himself was a man, like you and me, with the exception that He was without sin, even though He was tempted like every one of us. But one thing impacted Jesus deeply and caused Him to stand out from everyone else, making Him the prototype of the new man. It is the Word His heavenly Father spoke over Him, "**You are My Son, whom I love**" **(Mark 1:11)**.

As much as Jesus, the carpenter's son and itinerant preacher was misunderstood, despised, and rejected, this Word stuck with Him and fell deep into His heart. "**You are my Son, whom I love!**" It radically affected Him and brought Him into an abundance of life, a fullness of manhood, and a new anointing. It was the Word He ultimately leaned on when He went to Calvary as the Lamb of God, becoming the sacrifice that bore our sins. He, who was without sin, said, "I am the One to blame! Spit at Me! Beat Me up! Lash Me! Nail Me to the cross! Take it all out on Me! I am the scapegoat for the world!"

When God spoke to Him, **"You are My Son, whom I love!"** it propelled the carpenter's son from Nazareth into His position of authority as the prototype of a new man. In the end, God was able to say: "This is my Son, and I am giving Him the name that is above every name" (see Philippians 2:9).

Nothing in the world can empower a person like a father saying, "You are my daughter! You are My son!" It would revolutionize your heart if you could grasp the reality of what it means to be a daughter or a son of God. That is the good news to the poor. Do we understand this? It is good news for the poor who are still thinking, "I am just not right the way I am. There is no place for me in this world. If I would cease to exist, no one would really miss me. What could I possibly accomplish, with my lousy grades, with my poor training, with my social background, coming from a broken family?" And yet so often we fail to convey the good news to the poor! They will not be able to take a stand and become sons and daughters unless they find the Father's heart and hear the Father speak this message into their hearts.

There is no use in just being good people; that in itself will not change us. It is not about being good. Even being a faithful church attendee will not bring about real transformation. We need to become daughters and sons of God. Only the nobility of this status will ultimately transform us and make us new.

Sons and Daughters of the Father

The Key to Healing

This is the key to healing for our personality. It is the key for men to become real men. It is the key for women to become real women. It is the key for young people to rise up, knowing what the Father has spoken over them: "You are My son! You are My daughter!" Do we understand what this means? The living God says: "I want to be your Father! You are My daughter, My son! As sure as Jesus is My Son, you are My son, My daughter as well! No less! You legally are My child. You are entering into the inheritance that I, the Father, am giving to you. You are a co-heir with your brother, Christ Jesus." Just imagine your heart really grasping the message of Almighty God, the Creator of heaven and earth saying, "You are My son!"

Somebody might be sitting there, his head bowed, and his hair covering his face like a curtain, pondering, "I must have fallen off the bandwagon somewhere." But suddenly God appears and says, "Look at Me! Look into My eyes!" He gently parts that curtain of hair, telling him, "Son, look into My eyes! Don't you know you're My son? Don't you know you're My daughter, if My Son Jesus is living in you? I have poured My Spirit into you and you are My son, My daughter." You will feel this cry welling up in your heart: "Father!" And, all of a sudden, your soul is enabled to sense this heart-to-heart relationship with the Father and there is a growing desire to draw near to Him, over and over again.

True Revolution

Can you see that only this experience will build us up on the inside? Nothing else will change us. Moral standards will not! Doctrinal statements will not! Saying no to drugs, abstinence from alcohol, avoiding trouble, as good as all of that may be, will not make us a new person. The only thing that will ultimately change us is a revelation that we are a son or daughter of God.

We need to know that we are a son or daughter of God. Sons and daughters, who know that God is their Father and who receive their dignity from Him alone, will stir up a revolution in this world. They know, "I must be all right the way I am, otherwise God wouldn't keep telling me: You are My daughter, you are My son!" You will no longer be under men's jurisdiction, or even worse, your own jurisdiction. Your heart will no longer torment you because you despise yourself and would like to be different. God is telling you, "Look at Me. Just look into My eyes! If you received My Son into your heart and if you allow Me to make Myself at home in your life, then you are My son, My daughter! Leave it to Me to transform you into a person who can represent Me to the world. I will turn you into someone who radiates My love amidst good and evil people, amidst righteous and unrighteous people, amidst people who are thankful and people who are unthankful."

That's revolution! If God, through His call, led Jesus into such an abundance of human life, such an authority to fulfill His task, and such a powerful gentleness, then He will raise you up as well. His goal is not to make us stand out, but to make us genuinely human. You may succeed in sports or in the music business, but true greatness comes only through being truly human, and by being the image of our God. It means being His sons and daughters, seeing our Father's world through His eyes of love. That is just absolutely marvelous!

Sons and Daughters of the Father

For this reason, the Lord is pouring out His Spirit, the Spirit of the Father, abundantly once again. Let us not forget that He is at the same time the Spirit of the Son. Once He enters into your life, He brings the Fatherhood of God with Him who calls you into being. The Spirit will cry out within you: "You are the son, you are the daughter of the Father!" And your spirit will cry out in response: "Father! Father! Change my life, Father! Here I am, Your son, Your daughter! Raise me up!" I am so enthusiastic about what God is doing in these days! I am thrilled by how God calls His sons and daughters.

It fills my heart with joy to see Him calling messed-up men, who have been suffering from unhealthy relationships with women for many years and those who just could not value their spouses. All these men heard in their past was, "You are not acceptable the way you are. If only you could be like Jim or Joe!" But all of a sudden these men hear the Father say, "Look at Me!" Then the Father speaks into the life of these torn-up men, "You are My son and I am your Father!" Oh, you should observe these guys turn into sons. They receive an entirely new sense of dignity and it changes their inmost being, as well as their outward appearance, and enables them to become real men.

As a result, the quarrelling and bickering, the strife and contention, the tug-of-war at home ends because their spouses start to realize, "There's something changing in my husband! I need to hurry now or else I might be left behind!" Now these wives are encouraged to run and to hear it for themselves, "You are My daughter!" Sometimes it is the wife who hears and responds first, while he is the one to rush behind and jump on the train.

Father

Let us open our hearts once again to hear the Spirit of the Father. Let us stand before the Father as men and women, full of needs, who are sensing that we have not yet grasped what it means to be fully human, the way God intended us to be. We have not yet come to a place where we are truly sons and daughters of our heavenly Father. God wants to raise us up, proclaiming over our lives, "You are My son! You are My daughter!" Only this will make us whole and allow the love of God to be able to flow right through us.

Once you are a son or a daughter of God, He will surely lead people your way that you have been trying to avoid. These are the tests probing us to see if we really are His sons and daughters, and to see if we are able to take some criticism with a good attitude. This is just one example, but these are wonderful opportunities for practice. One day, a person came up to me and said, "Pastor, I listened to one of your tapes just recently, but quite honestly, I turned it off pretty quickly." I answered him, "You see, that's why I do not like to listen to my tapes myself."

We are no longer walking through a dangerous minefield in this world. Being sons and daughters of the Father, we have already reached home. The world belongs to our Father. As His children, we are walking on the property of our heavenly Father, carrying His love into the world. No doubt, this is a challenge, but it surely is fun as well!

Prayer

Father, You created Adam from a lump of clay, and he was good and perfect. You brought him to life by breathing Your Fatherhood into him, proclaiming "You are My son!" and he became a living being.

Sons and Daughters of the Father

Father, we are created beings, we have life, strength, vision, and dreams in us. And yet many of us need this breath of the Father once again. We need the wind of the Spirit to come over us once more, the breath of the Father proclaiming over us, "You are My daughter! You are My son! Stand to your feet! Look at Me! Look into My eyes! I want to be available to you and lead you! I will fight for you! Let Me make you a man, let Me make you a woman after My own image, so that streams of love would flow through you. Then you will no longer classify people and divide them into those you like and those you dislike, but you will be like the wind that reaches everyone." The wind does not ask, "Is it okay for you if I am blowing at you?" It just blows over people. In the same way, our love will ooze off of us wherever we go, without asking whether people like it or not!

So we ask You: Come Holy Spirit and bring the breath of the Father once again! Breathe over us once again the Creator's breath that helps us to rise up. Carve deep into our hearts that we are indeed sons and daughters, let us hear the approval of the Father: "You are pleasing to Me, just the way you are. I am so pleased with you! Just allow Me to fill you with My love! Allow Me to give you a steadfast heart and a fearless spirit! Let Me open the eyes of your inner man, so you can see what I want to show you. Let Me open your inner ears!"

Come, Holy Spirit! Pour Yourself out over Your people! Bless Your people with Your Fatherhood! Flow, Holy Spirit, into everything that is dried up and withered. Bring the Father's love with You! Bring the Father's joy and laughter! We know You are holy, holy, holy. But at the same time You are a Father who rejoices over His children! There is laughter at Your table. I praise You and honor You, Holy Spirit, for removing our yokes in spite of the poverty and lowliness of the human nature. Come, Father, breathe on Your sons and daughters. Breathe on them!

Father

We praise You, Father, that the time is coming where we will rejoice over our God once again. We will no longer be downcast, but Your people will be full of joy for having such a Father, such a Lord and Savior, Jesus Christ, who put His Spirit into us, so the Father's love can once again flow freely in our lives and through us into the world.

EIGHT

Rooted in the Father
The Divine "Visa"

"In a surge of anger I hid My face from you for a moment, but with everlasting kindness I will have compassion on you,' says the Lord your Redeemer.

To Me this is like the days of Noah, when I swore that the waters of Noah would never again cover the earth. So now I have sworn not to be angry with you, never to rebuke you again.

Though the mountains be shaken and the hills be removed, yet my unfailing love for you will not be shaken nor my covenant of peace be removed,' says the Lord, who has compassion on you.

'O afflicted city, lashed by storms and not comforted, I will build you with stones of turquoise, your foundations with sapphires.

I will make your battlements of rubies, your gates of sparkling jewels, and all your walls of precious stones.

All your sons will be taught by the Lord, and great will be your children's peace.

In righteousness you will be established: Tyranny will be far from you; you will have nothing to fear. Terror will be far removed; it will not come near you" (Isaiah 54:8-14).

God Is Refining the Foundations

This is a very prophetic word for our time. God is about to refine our foundations and firmly establish them. The most precious materials are mentioned here—substances that have a very special sparkle to them and cannot be destroyed.

At first, He promises, **"In a surge of anger**—for a brief moment— **I hid My face from you...but with everlasting kindness I will have compassion on you,' says the Lord your Redeemer.** Like in the days of Noah, **"when I swore** (with the rainbow that I put into the sky) **that the waters of Noah would never again cover the earth. So now I have sworn not to be angry with you, never to rebuke you again. Though the mountains be shaken and the hills be removed, yet my unfailing love for you will not be shaken, nor my covenant of peace be removed"** (Isaiah 54:9-10). He then follows with the prophetic word about the foundations: **"I will build your foundations with precious stones."**

In the epistle to the Hebrews, God said He would once again shake all things (see Hebrews 12:26). We are approaching this time, where the foundations will be shaken. In fact, it has already begun. God said He would test and refine everything through fire. John the Baptist put it like this: **"... after me will come one who is more powerful than I, whose sandals I am not fit**

to carry. He will baptize you with the Holy Spirit and with fire" (Matthew 3:11).

We have seen wonderful times of blessing and refreshing in the Holy Spirit. The love of God was flowing; people could laugh again and receive healing through the joy that the Holy Spirit poured into their hearts. Emotional pain that used to be locked up deep inside was suddenly released to flow to the cross. People were able to let go of their rigid desire for control in their own lives and in their churches and were set free to do things they normally would not do. All of a sudden we were able to burst through walls of self-control and become fools for Jesus.

Baptized with Fire

But we will also be going through a fire, even in this time! There is not just the fire of hell, but there is also the fire of the Spirit! There are people who are courageous enough to pray, "God, baptize me with fire!" We know this will not happen by our own strength. We want to be careful not to be a big mouth like Peter who boldly declared, "Even if I have to die with you, I will never disown you!" (see Matthew 26:35) or like John and James, the sons of thunder who said, "Yes, we can drink Your cup!" (see Matthew 20:22) For sure, we cannot! We cannot do it unless Jesus, who is stronger than the world, is in us. We can only do it by the power of the Holy Spirit and by grace. However, by the grace of having Jesus in us, we can scale walls. And by this grace, we can also be baptized by fire.

Many have already gone through baptisms of fire. Whoever shares this experience knows that these are special times of grace! It is a tremendous privilege when God, by His grace, leads us through these baptisms of fire. The Father knows when we are ready for them.

Father

Everything that is supposed to last has to go through fire. The shining colors of the glaze on a piece of pottery will only show after they have gone through the heat of an oven. After this procedure, the glaze is no longer just a coat of paint that can be scratched off easily, it is hard as stone. Whenever we go through these trials of fire, we experience the glory of God.

Rooted in the Father

We are entering into a time of serious shaking that will be such a season of trial and refining by fire. To prepare us, God is going to lay an immovable foundation once again. Being rooted in God's Fatherhood will be part of that foundation. Paul mentions this in Ephesians 3:14, where he says: **"For this reason I kneel before the Father, from whom His whole family in heaven and on earth derives its name" (Ephesians 3:14-15)**. He goes on to talk about us being **"rooted and established"** in the Father's love which is revealed in Jesus. If this foundation is to be laid once again, we need a revelation of the Father. The Father needs to be deeply engraved into our hearts, our souls, and our innermost beings. Everything in us needs to know, "Yes, I am rooted in the heavenly Father!"

We can come to the Father with ragged clothes and with everything that is still unfinished in our lives because we are aware of the fact that as His children, we are in a process of transformation as long as there is breath in us. We will always be lacking. Only when we see Jesus will we become perfect. Standing before Him, we will be transformed into His image in an instant, and from then on we will be like Him. Nevertheless we can come to the throne of grace even now, with all our inner voids and flaws. We can nestle up to the Father knowing that we will find rest in Him. He wants to be our secure dwelling place, where no one can chase us away. God said, "I will no longer be angry with you. I am with you. You are My daughter; you are My son!" This is what we need to know deep, deep down in our spirit, in our soul, and in our gut.

God's Visa

If you want to travel to China, Mongolia, or many other countries, you need a visa. Sometimes they can be very complicated to obtain. The word visa, like video, is based on the Latin word "to see," "to look at" or "to behold something." As much as applying for a visa oftentimes involves a lot of bureaucratic paperwork, the virtual act of looking requires some time in itself. Every officer has to look at the application, many times very closely. When God was in the process of creating the world, "He saw all that He had made and it was very good," which we read in Genesis 1 more than once. Why would God even bother? Is God Himself not the One who is at work? Could He not just assume that if He, the perfect One, creates something, it will surely turn out perfectly fine? Nevertheless, He issues His "visa" for every single one of His works! Even today He is looking at each one of His creatures stating, "How beautiful this is!"

Every artist keeps stepping back from his work to take an overall look at it. He will approach it again, adjusting the easel just a little so the light can fall on the picture at the right angle. He looks at it full of joy because he can already envision the finished work in his mind. Even though it is his creation, he can see that there is much more potential in his work than he had ever imagined. When God looked at His finished creation, He was awestruck. It burst out of Him, "This is not just good, it is very good! I have made something really magnificent!" (see Genesis 1:31). This is Almighty God speaking! He is the Creator, the Master Artist. Whenever we are creative, in worship music, visual arts, or dancing, all the creativity flowing from within us is an expression of His heart.

When I was in Mongolia, I saw a "yak" for the first time in my life. To me, it was the oddest creature. It seemed to be a mixture between a horse and a cow. But God saw this animal. In fact, He looked at it for a long time, like He looked at everything else He had created—and to Him it was just beautiful! He might have even thought, "Let's play a little trick on the zoologists, something that will mess them up real good!" This is just beautiful.

The act of beholding is an essential part of creation. Only after a close, final examination will the artist approve his finished work and say, "That's it. That's exactly the way I intended it to look like. Now it is ready to be released." Then he puts his signature on it—his "visa." Rembrandt and other artists often paused for years, adjusting certain sections of a painting over and over again.

For this reason, God gave us the second account of creation (see Genesis 2), dealing in particular with the creation of the woman. Of course, her creation is mentioned in the first account as well, but in the beginning of the second account, we can read that God wanted to make some improvements because He felt that there was still something missing for the creation of man to become perfect. So He made a woman from one of Adam's ribs. Can you see what is happening here? Whenever God decides to launch a second attempt, He creates something that surpasses His former work. When God brought Eve to Adam, Adam exploded with enthusiasm: "This is great! Finally! This is now bone of my bones and flesh of my flesh!" (see Genesis 2:23) That is God's personality!

All of Us Need the Visa

We need the divine visa to really know, "It is well!" You will constantly struggle with insecurity and life will be hard on you unless you have the visa of God, that divine stamp of approval on your life. The visa establishes beyond any doubt that somebody out there is saying: *"Yes, you are the one! I love you and I want you to be here!"* Even Jesus Himself needed the divine visa! The Father gave His first approval to Jesus on the day of His birth, when the heavens opened and the angels were singing **"Glory to God in the highest..." (Luke 2:14)** as a prophetic sign, a divine visa.

At His baptism, the heavens opened again, and a voice was heard: **"This is my Son, whom I love; with him I am well pleased" (Matthew 3:17).** That is a visa! Later on the mount of transfiguration, God made the same statement: **"This is my Son, whom I love; with him I am well pleased. Listen to him!" (Matthew 17:5).** Finally God publicly confirmed the prayer of His Son in a thunderous proclamation: **"I have glorified it, and will glorify it again (John 12:28).**

Jesus had a visa from His Father! He revealed the Father to us all so we could also receive this divine visa, the Father's stamp of approval on our lives. For this reason we are being sealed with the Holy Spirit. The Spirit of God in us is the seal, the visa stating, "You are the one!" Having been given this seal of approval, we can be totally assured in our hearts that God is indeed interested in us personally.

Father

I grew up in a Christian home. I absorbed the faith early on in my life and I got "saved" at least twenty or thirty times. Everybody thought I was a good boy. Later on, I became a pastor, preaching the gospel. Yet I never felt like I had that visa; I was a Christian, but I was not really "born again." We need to be born of the Holy Spirit. I am not talking about some sort of technicality here, a legal act decreed on paper like an adoption. We need to be born by the Spirit of God, not by flesh and blood (see John 1:13). Can you see that this is a creative act? You are begotten by the Holy Spirit to be a daughter, to be a son of the Most High. The Holy Spirit is then bearing witness within you. He is the One testifying to your spirit that you are indeed His child, a legitimate child, begotten by God Himself (see Romans 8:16). This is how you receive the visa of God, proclaiming over you: "I approve of you. You are a masterpiece of Mine! You are beautifully made! My daughter! My son!"

The Work of Jesus

What did Jesus do when He knelt down in front of the adulterous woman, writing in the sand and approving her instead of condemning her? By saying, "Go and sin no more," (see John 8:3-11) He issued her the divine visa. What did He give to the Samaritan woman at the well? He gave her His visa: "You shall live! I am giving you a source of living water that will flow into eternity!" (see John 4:7-30) What did He offer the disciples, especially Peter, in spite of his betrayal: "You are approved! Everything will be all right! You are Peter, and on this rock I will build My church!" (see Matthew 16:17-18) That is God's personality. He can restore us and make us new, even after Satan has brought hell and destruction over us. But we have to know deep in our spirits that we have been granted a divine visa. If I have stumbled, I can get up again. I can call on Jesus, His blood will purify me, and I will be able to move on.

Rooted in the Father

You have to have this visa or you will always feel insecure in life. And not only in life, but the same will be true for the church. There are way too many Christians attending churches who do not have that visa yet! Before you are due to appear in court, you need to know for sure that your sins are forgiven and that your debt is cancelled. Once you have the assurance that you are a child of God, no one will be able to steal it away from you. No longer will you say that you hope to see Jesus someday. You will know it for a fact because you carry the seal of God. In the midst of all the temptations we keep falling into over and again, each one of us needs to be confident that he is God's child, accepted by Him. I need to know that God is telling me, "I have sworn never to leave you nor forsake you! Never!" (see Joshua 1:5). God does not lie—when He made this promise that was exactly what He meant to say. The very foundation of our existence rests in the blood of Jesus. Jesus Himself is the foundation.

We need to ask ourselves again: "Do I have that visa? Am I sealed with the Holy Spirit? Do I know it for a fact?" If you do not, you need to come to that point of assurance. You need to have this divine visa when times of shaking come. People may question your salvation or you may be tempted and even fall every once in a while. But even in the midst of a storm, you will know that the Father admitted you. The Holy Spirit, the wonderful Counselor, who leads you into all truth, will keep whispering to you: "You are saved! Who could harm you—God is for you!"

And to spiritual leaders, He says, **"Here is my servant, whom I uphold, my chosen one in whom I delight; I will put my Spirit on him and he will bring justice to the nations"** (Isaiah 42:1). As a leader, you are in particular need of this seal. If you are approved by God Himself, people may badmouth you as much as they want to, but God will make clear that your leadership is directly from Him and not from men.

Churches Need to Be Solidly Founded on the Fatherhood of God

I firmly believe that whole churches need to have the visa of the Father. They have to be founded on His Fatherhood. Churches are being refined because God wants their foundation to be made up of turquoise and sapphires once again. We cannot afford to build our churches on sand any longer. Great visions and bold dreams are not enough. Just dreaming of establishing a certain number of churches within a specific time frame will not do. So many have failed because they envisioned their own and not God's ideas! These dreams had no foundation to them. If churches are not solidly grounded on the foundation of turquoise and sapphire—on the Fatherhood of God, the cross and blood of Jesus Christ, and on God's grace and truth—they will vanish. Times are changing and churches will be shaken as well.

We need to come back to the Father, even as entire church bodies. We need to be solidly rooted in the Fatherhood of God, in the unshakable knowledge that **"the Father... is greater than all!" (John 10:29)**. The Scripture makes it quite clear that we must enter into the rest of God (see Hebrews 4). Only when we are close to the Father will we find rest. We need to be on His lap. Why was Jesus radiating with such serenity amidst a world of madness? He was the only One who was never sidetracked. He did not think He had to fight the Romans or anything else in this world. He never tried to be anyone else but Himself; He did not raise His voice in the streets; He did not snuff out the smoldering wick—nor did He break the bruised reed. When He met a blind man, the Savior of the world took the time to make an ointment of dirt and saliva and put it on his eyes. With another blind man, He walked hand-in-hand out of the village. He was a man of serenity, walking in the Father's rest.

You can always tell if a church is walking in rest or whether it is full of upheaval. A church must be at rest in God, it must rest from its own works. Only then can it enter into the works prepared by God, the place of anointing and true destiny. Many churches are like the racing carriages with twelve horses that we so often see in Western movies. The pastor is sitting on the coach-box, cracking his whip. Whenever things seem to get out of hand, he will start making his way to the front by jumping from horse to horse in order to reach the first team, until finally he falls off one of the horses. We have to remind ourselves that we are not actors in a wild movie. In fact, we were never supposed to act anything out.

Because we are citizens of the kingdom, we can enter into the place of rest assigned to us by God Himself. The most awesome works are done out of this resting place! Out of His place of rest, Jesus started making His way to the cross on Golgotha. In Him, we can seize hope that there is a future for us in the kingdom of God. Whoever represents Jesus is able to impart **"streams of living water" (John 7:38)** simply because Jesus lives in him. You cannot explain it, but if somebody who is full of Jesus enters a room, significant things will happen.

When the great evangelist Charles Finney walked down a street, people started falling under the power of the Spirit. It was the presence of God on him. When the shadow of the apostles fell on the sick, they were healed. What else could have accomplished these miracles but the power of God on these men? If we start entering into His rest and Jesus takes form in us, God will be able to do through us the things that really matter.

The Younger Sons and the Older Brothers

Many "younger sons" set out full of enthusiasm to build something new, something different. They were dreaming of glorious times. Thousands asked God for their share of the heritage and left with hearts full of vision to finally refurbish the old vessels of their established churches and denominations. In the same way, many of the young charismatic churches took the riches of the Father—the Word of God, the Holy Spirit, and the fellowship of the brothers and sisters—and just took off.

We must come back to the Father. There cannot be any life that is not rooted, established, and secured in the Father's rest. But if we rest in Him, we will move cities, regions, and even whole nations because God will burst forth with tremendous power. Do not worry, you will certainly not be laid off. He will put you to work and you will experience the kingdom of God. We will grow beyond our limits, but we must first come back to the Father.

Further, we need to have compassion with each other, just like the Father has been compassionate with us. He never bursts out in anger or says in a nagging tone, "See! I knew it! You should have…!" Rather, He ran out to meet the younger son and put His arms around him (see Luke 15:20). This is how we should learn to treat each other in the body of Christ. Whenever churches split, become enslaved, or fall into poverty, let us go out to meet them and help them up. Let us love on them and encourage them. Let us be their friends, their brothers and sisters. Let us welcome them and offer them our fellowship. It takes the heart of God for us to be able to do that. We need this kind of encouragement because there are so many discouraged and hurting people in the body of Christ. When God goes out to meet His bruised, homecoming son, He encourages him and says, "It is so good to have you back." Such a warm embrace often brings people to a point of repentance and enables them to admit, "I was wrong; I want to enter into God's rest again."

But the older brothers, those who stayed in the Father's house all the while, need to come to the Father as well, even though they are convinced, "We are so smart. We just kept the balance and stayed in the mainstream." They did not neglect the Holy Spirit. They took a little from all of the waves that washed over the body of Christ, from spiritual warfare to healing the sick. They even allow a little deliverance ministry behind closed doors here and there, if it seems unavoidable. They never go overboard and they never expose any rough edges. Everything about them is geared for maximum efficiency and high-gloss appearance. But that does not bring us life either.

The older brothers must also come back to the Father, even if they never really left Him—even if they always wanted to do things right while they were serving God. Yet they are not fully immersed in His stream of life. We may be standing on the riverbanks with rolled-up pants, getting our feet wet, but it is time to go deeper into the stream of life! We will get there as we ground ourselves solidly in the Father's heart.

The Holy Spirit will do that for us; it is His work. I cannot impart the Father's love to you, I can only testify to what the Father has done in my own heart. Since I have received my

Father

Father's seal of approval, His visa, I can live. Something inside of me has found peace. In the past, I used to kick-start all kinds of activities whenever an exciting new idea entered my mind. Today I do not have to do that anymore. I have come to a place of rest in my Father. If we are rooted in the Father's heart, He will keep giving us work to do and He will make room for us.

Niklaus von Flüe

There is a peculiar saint in our own Swiss history. His name is Niklaus von Flüe (spoken "fon Flue-eh")—a man who had come to rest at the Father's heart. Through this man, who for a period of almost twenty years ate and drank practically nothing, God issued a tremendous call of repentance to the wealthy, complacent church of those days. His example was a prophetic proclamation that God's people ought to live on the grace of God and on His Word, not on the selling of indulgences and fundraising. Through him, God declared, "My grace is sufficient! My Word is sufficient! Man may be satisfied by My Word and My fellowship alone!" That was something unique. God used this man in a powerful way to influence a whole nation.

NINE

The "Real Father"

A Personal Relationship with the Living God

"For this reason I kneel before the Father, from whom his whole family in heaven and on earth derives its name.

I pray that out of his glorious riches he may strengthen you with power through his Spirit in your inner being,

so that Christ may dwell in your hearts through faith. And I pray that you, being rooted and established in love,

may have power, together with all the saints, to grasp how wide and long and high and deep is the love of Christ,

and to know this love that surpasses knowledge—that you may be filled to the measure of all the fullness of God.

Now to him who is able to do immeasurably more than all we ask or imagine, according to his power that is at work within us,

**to him be glory in the Church and in Christ Jesus
throughout all generations, for ever and ever! Amen"
(Ephesians 3:14-21).**

Paul wrote this prayer of praise while he was incarcerated.
Thus it was written under circumstances that were not necessarily
conducive to contemplation of the lovingkindness of God. And
yet Paul was overwhelmed by the heart of God, the mystery of
His love and the mystery of Jesus Christ.

Germany Rocked by Crisis

My impression is that Germany in particular needs a special
touch from the "Father of all fatherhood," from the "real
Father." There were many fathers in the history of Germany,
some of whom took advantage of their position and misled and
deceived the German people. The current state of society in this
country also grieves me—the devaluation of marriage and the
destruction of family structures that has left so many men and
women with deep wounds of abandonment from the broken
homes they grew up in—the devaluation of authority caused by
highly esteemed and prominent figures who have been involved
in scandals; and the ravaging feelings of shame, rooted in the
dishonor that the country you loved and served experienced. In
Switzerland, we just went through such a time of dishonor where
our nation was debased and put in the spotlight of the world. It
was very humiliating.

Standing on the Rock

We need to simply return to the Rock on which we can stand
securely. It seems to me that sometimes we have lost our very
foundation. We still know a lot about the faith and there is a

strong basis of tradition left in the Lutheran church where I used to be a pastor, but it looks very much like the ground has vanished from beneath our feet. We are no longer standing on the Rock. One thing has to be clarified though: This Rock does not primarily consist of doctrinal statements. Above all else, it is centered on a personal, heart-to-heart relationship with God. We can sum up the entire gospel in the following statement of Jesus: **"I am in the Father, and that the Father is in Me" (John 14:10).** That is the essence of the gospel. It is actually that simple.

I in You and You in Me

If we really love one another from the depth of our hearts and if love is flowing through us to our neighbor, our spouse, our children, or to our parents, there is always a secret to it. It has something to do with the other person being in my heart and me being in his or her heart. What is true marriage after all? It is my spouse being in my heart and me being in my spouse's heart. That is the secret of love. It is not about submitting to certain external forms or rules. It is about abiding in each other's heart. If we have the assurance that we are loved, all it takes is a little gesture, a brief touch, even a glance to let the other person know: "I have a place in her heart and she has a place inside me." That is all we want and ultimately need.

Often we turn our Christian lives into something very complicated. We want to be good Christians according to the letter and try to do all kinds of things to please Him—pray more, read the Bible more, get more involved in ministry, or even sell our houses and work full-time for the Lord. None of this is wrong in itself, but let us push all of it over to the side for a moment and ask ourselves: "Does God live in my heart, and am I living in His?" That is what love is all about! What do you think is the joy of God's heart—to mark in a book how many hours you prayed or read your Bible or for Him to simply live in you?

No Pressure

Some time ago I attended an intercessors' camp. There were certain camp rules to which you had to agree. For example, every participant was supposed to pray four hours a day. If you wanted to be a real prayer warrior, you consecrated your nights to prayer as well. So I got up at two or three o'clock in the morning to pray. I prayed and prayed and prayed until I became totally depressed. Finally, my throat was so sore that I lost my voice and could not preach anymore. In the middle of the night, there I was, moaning and groaning and everything else I could think of, in order to be a powerful intercessor.

However, God did not seem particularly inclined to honor my efforts. Instead of putting a special anointing on my voice, He decided to slow me down until I was ready to stop showing off and ask Him instead: "God, do You even want me to do this?" Finally, I surrendered and said, "Okay God, I am not the mighty prayer warrior I wanted to be. I am not a hero who spends his nights in prayer and goes to bed after hours of intercession, just to be back on his feet at six o'clock in the morning, convinced of what a wonderful guy I really am!" My depression lifted instantly and I felt fine again.

What was John's secret, whom the Bible calls **"the disciple whom Jesus loved?" (John 13:23)** His secret was actually very plain: Jesus was in his heart and he was in the heart of Jesus. Only for this reason was he courageous enough to stay with Jesus until the very end, even standing under His cross. This can only happen if Jesus is in your heart and you are in His. If that is the reality of your life, there is no room for fear: **"Perfect love drives out fear" (I John 4:18).** We need to return to this solid foundation: He in me and I in Him. We must come back to the point where we are able to cry with joy and delight that Jesus is in me and that I am in the heart of Jesus, the King of kings.

Read John 17 every once in a while, where Jesus tells the disciples that the Father is in Him, as He is in us, and we are in Him. In His so-called high priestly prayer, Jesus presented a final overview of the essence of the gospel: It is all about love—to love God with all our hearts, all of our souls, all of our minds, and with all of our strength; and out of the love the Lord has given us, to love our neighbor as ourselves.

The Real Father Overwhelmed with Compassion

To me, a real father is compassionate. Whenever God introduces Himself to people, He always reveals Himself as "compassionate and gracious, compassionate and gracious, compassionate and gracious" (see Exodus 33:19). If God is our Creator and Father, then He will be gracious and compassionate in a manner that is way beyond our imagination. Remember how you feel about your own children. You love them and if they happen to hurt themselves, you tend to feel the pain much stronger than they themselves do. God knows us down to the deepest parts of our hearts. Your life is like an open book to Him. He knows every thought that comes to your mind and every word on your lips. Therefore, He is always overwhelmed with compassion for us, His children.

Jesus wept over people, which shows us how compassionately God cares about us. He knows how we are doing and what we are dealing with. If we are counseling people and ministering to them, God's compassion will sometimes overwhelm us. It always amazes me how touched I am after I have talked to people for only a few minutes, listening to them and trying to understand how they might feel. My heart goes out to them, and I am so full of compassion that I could actually start crying. But all we ever get to see of other people's feelings is the tip of the iceberg. God looks down into the deepest places. He sees the generations that have gone before you and those that will come after you. Everything is totally transparent to Him. That is why He is compassionate beyond all limits! Whatever moves our hearts makes His heart overflow with compassion.

A Bow in the Sky

After the flood, the entire magnificent and awesome creation was totally destroyed. Only mud and chaos remained. All of the splendor God had created in His passion was ruined. All that was left were the pairs of animals and the handful of people who had been saved through the ark. At this point, Noah offered up a sacrifice to God, bowing his knees and lifting up his hands. He thanked the Creator for rescuing all of them through the forty-day ordeal of darkness, even though they had been trapped in a wooden dungeon that was worse than the stomach of the fish that Jonah had to endure. Outside you could hear the rain, pelting on the roof. Later on, there was only a daunting silence; inside the ark were the noises of animals, locked into this floating crate. All they could do was to feed the animals and wander around, warming and comforting each other until they were finally able to open a window and let a raven fly out. When those days were over, Noah began building his altar. He lifted his hands and the smoke of his sacrifice rose into the sky. Then

The "Real Father"

Scripture declares, **"The Lord smelled the pleasing aroma..."** **(Genesis 8:21).** God was gripped with compassion and all the frustration over His destroyed creation seemed to vanish. At this point, the Bible says that God decided in His heart:

> **"Never again will I curse the ground because of man, even though every inclination of his heart is evil from childhood. And never again will I destroy all living creatures, as I have done.**
>
> **As long as the earth endures, seedtime and harvest, cold and heat, summer and winter, day and night will never cease" (Genesis 8:21-22).**

And to emphasize His commitment, God put a marvelous rainbow in the clouds, making a covenant with Noah (see Genesis 9:12-17). What an amazing sign of God's mercy and compassion!

Compassion on a Murderer

Think of king Ahab, who took away a vineyard from a poor fellow, initiated a conspiracy against him with the help of his wife and a couple of false witnesses, and in the end, had him stoned to death (see I Kings 21). One day after the dirty business was taken care of, Ahab took a little walk on his new property. It was a little after lunch and his stomach was full—he was probably still sucking on a mint candy. Suddenly, a prophet approached him, declaring, "What a miserable creature you are! You killed a man for a bunch of cabbage heads!" Immediately the king was filled with remorse. Amazingly enough, God gave new orders to the prophet: "Go back and tell him that I will delay judgment so that it will not strike during his lifetime."

Father

What an example of God's compassion! It takes just a tiny spark, a spark of someone crying out to God, and the heart of God overflows with His boundless compassion over our destitute and deficient condition. A tiny spark will ignite God's mercy over the limited perspective we have in this life, coveting our neighbor's yard to add it to our own, just to plant a couple of cabbages and try a different spot for our favorite lawn chair. King Ahab really believed this was all that counted in life. But God had compassion on this murderer who had his neighbor's blood still on his hands.

Or think of Cain who beat his brother to death, staining creation with human blood for the first time. Cain cried out to God, "Now they'll kill me wherever I go—I am outlawed" (see Genesis 4:14). But God, in His compassion, put a mark on Cain and declared, "Not so; if anyone kills Cain, he will suffer vengeance seven times over. You are under My protection" (see Genesis 4:15). Over and over again we see the compassion of God.

Jesus—God's Overflowing Compassion

What tremendous compassion we see in the Man Jesus of Nazareth, the carpenter and Son of God! Such compassion! Wherever we look in the gospels, we find Jesus responding to every single person crying out to Him and to every need that people presented to Him. (see Luke 18:40). That makes me think of the way I manage my time. In leadership training, we are taught: "Don't waste your time on people who are problem-oriented, but reach out to those who are able to focus on solutions." And since we have learned to be time-conscious in order to fulfill our callings, we keep asking ourselves: "Is the person who is addressing me at the moment really a 'key figure' for my calling? Is it someone in leadership?"

As important as it may be to ask ourselves such questions, look at what Jesus did. He had the most important calling of all—to become the Savior of the world and to fulfill the work of redemption that would forever impact world history. And yet people came and brought in a blind man to Him, pleading with Jesus to heal him. Jesus did not feel sidetracked by their requests. He was overwhelmed with compassion for this man because He knew the rejection he was facing and his feelings of being a burden to everyone around him. Now his family and friends had brought him to Jesus with the hope of finally getting that burden off their own backs. Maybe, they reasoned, Jesus would heal him so he could take care of himself in the future. But Jesus looked at him, full of compassion. He took him by the hand and led him away from all of those people, just to spend a few moments with him alone (see Mark 8:23). He, the King of kings on His way to the cross, fulfilling the greatest mission anyone could ever have on this earth.

May I Come in and Stay with You?

We have lost sight of God because we chose to turn our backs on Him. But this "lost" God still decided to come to us; He comes to His own, knocks at the doors of our hearts and says to every one of us, "Open the door for Me!" For this reason, the Bible says that Jesus had nowhere to lay His head (see Matthew 8:20). That is a prophetic statement. Of course, Jesus had houses where He could visit, but there was no place to really lay His head. This can only happen in our hearts. God can only rest His head in our hearts and we can only find rest if we lay our heads in His heart. It blows me away to think that God is standing at the door of my life, asking, "Can I come in and stay with you?" What an awesome sense of dignity we can draw from this reality! Jesus said, "The Father and I want to come and move in with you through the Holy Spirit" (see John 13:23).

Prayer

Holy Spirit, please give us a revelation of what it means for the God of heaven and earth to live in us and to transform us into His image. Please reveal to us how God is modeling His very own character into us and how He lets His power, His life, His freedom, His compassion, and His love to be reflected in us. He lives in us in spite of all the hurting places in our hearts that still require healing. He lives in us and even chooses to be in hardened hearts that have not yet been softened. God is resting His head on your hardened heart, drenching it with His tears and with the blood of Jesus, until you surrender all the disappointments and bitterness to Him and He can give you a new heart made of flesh. What a privilege! This is the only solid foundation to stand and to live on.

*Jesus, You reminded us that we need to build the houses of our lives on You, the solid Rock. If we don't, they will not be able to withstand the storms that are coming our way. I thank You, Lord, that You constantly go to deeper levels with us, until we are willing to expose our hearts to You and surrender all the things we don't understand and the experiences that have disappointed us. From this soil, the soil of our trust in the Father, true life will eventually spring up. There is no other name in heaven and on earth and under the earth, except for Your name, and in You we see the glory of the Father. On the cross, You revealed the glory of the Father to us. Your face was radiating with His glory when You pleaded, **"Father, forgive them,***

The "Real Father"

*for they do not know what they are doing!" (**Luke 23:34**) Or when You said: "**Father, into Your hands I commit my spirit!**" (**Luke 23:46**) When You spoke these words, the glory of the God of Abraham, Isaac and Jacob, the glory of the true Father shone through You. Jesus, we want to look into Your face and see the Father's heart reflected in it.*

We ask you: Come, Holy Spirit. Come and bring the Fathering Spirit, this solid Rock to our hearts. Only then our souls and spirits, our minds and emotions will be rooted and established in this love, and not in the quicksand of shallow experiences. Let our lives be God-rooted, rooted in You, deeply rooted in You! Holy Spirit lay this solid Father-foundation in us.

Father, I thank You for lifting Your countenance on us like You have done from the very beginning. Please lift Your countenance, the kind look of a Father and friend on everybody in this place now. Let Your face, Your Fatherly face shine when You see the children You created and for whom You gave Your life.

Jesus, touch our hearts deep within. I also pray for those who have doubts. Would You tell them: "Come, put your finger into My hands and feet and see for yourself that I have chosen you. Reach out your hand and put it into My side and see for yourself that I have chosen you. I gave everything for you, so I could say: You in Me and I in you."

TEN

The Father of Compassion

A Word to the "Older Son"

"**P**raise be to the God and Father of our Lord Jesus Christ, the Father of compassion and the God of all comfort" (II Corinthians 1:3).

"I Am Still Standing Outside..."

I want to say a few words to those who feel like there is some kind of screen between them and God, and who find themselves somehow standing on the outside. They hear the truth over and over again, but it just does not compute in their hearts. Deep inside of them is a cry of desperation: "Why not me, Lord?" They become even more desperate whenever they see others being touched by the presence of God in a powerful way and watch people shedding their tears or becoming radiant with joy, cheering, and dancing because they have been set free. But even if we do not share these experiences, we do not need to hide. We have to remember that we are their friends, brothers, and sisters, even if we still feel like we are standing behind a screen and the things we know in our heads do not seem to reach our hearts.

Father

It is my impression that we are dealing with the emotions of the "older brother" in the parable of the Prodigal Son (see Luke 15:25-32). He comes home from the fields, noticing the glittering party that was going on with music, dancing, and all the other festivities. They had even killed the fattened calf. Everybody in the house had been looking forward to feasting on the meat during the yearly celebration, when the harvest was brought in and the work for the year was done. Without even asking him, they had dished out the reward for the entire year's work to honor his little brother just because that jerk had finally come home. And now that older brother stands in front of the house raging with fury and deep frustration. I think many of us are dealing with this kind of disappointment. I am convinced that this is one of the issues with which western Christianity is struggling.

Europe—the "Older Brother"

It seems to me like God is coming out to meet the older brother at this time. God is coming from the huge glittering parties that are going on all over the world—massive evangelistic meetings, revivals in many countries where people are pouring in by the hundreds of thousands, even by the millions, and taking hold of the kingdom. Places like Africa, where Reinhard Bonnke is holding his open air crusades, or Argentina, or other countries where parties are going on and heaven seems to be killing the fattened calf to celebrate the harvest that is being gathered. Sometimes I wonder why God does not just turn His back on the spiritual misery of the western world once and for all. But He is coming to us from these parties in South America and Africa or other places to meet us, the older brothers and sisters in a Europe that used to be a Christian continent. He comes and talks to us like a Father.

The Father of Compassion

Once again, God is courting the older brothers and sisters whose faith is nothing but head knowledge, who live by regulations and derive their value from what they accomplish in ministry. They are carrying the burden of responsibility for broken people, churches, and ministries, but they themselves seem to get nothing. They might be dreaming of a "little goat," but it never happens. It just never seems to cross the Father's mind to come and tell them, "All right, son, here's a goat. Go and invite your friends for dinner and have a good time together."

The Father Is Speaking to the Defiant Child

Now that the Father stands right before you, He does not start counseling you; He simply says, "My child!" just as one would talk to a defiant or desperate child that is totally confused, stomping on the ground, and refusing to be comforted. Today, God is turning to us like a Father would turn to such a child, gently stroking his hair and telling him, "Child, My child, everything I have is yours."

Father God is pleading with you, the desperate child that is screaming and stamping deep inside, banging your head against the wall. You may be going over all of the calculations again and again, the accounts of your Christian life, while God is trying to tell you. "My dear child, please rejoice and be happy now." Is it not amazing that our God is pleading with us to share His joy over people who are breaking through to a new life, taking off their old rags and putting on the clothes of righteousness? Our God is begging you to let go of your attitude, your foot-stomping, and your complaining, "Father, I will not come in until I feel like it." God is taking that raging, stomping child by the hand, saying, "Come on in with Me. Please, do Me the favor! Come in and rejoice with Me."

Father

Maybe your healing will begin when you start to address that despairing, screaming child within you: "All right, now let's grasp the Father's hand. Let's rejoice together with God and share in His joy. We do not want to leave God out in the cold. We will not leave Him alone with His pain and joy any longer."

We left Him alone in the Garden of Gethsemane because we all fell asleep. We left Him alone on the cross. We left Him alone in that moment of deepest darkness when the Father forsook Him. But now, He is standing before us once more. The time has come for God to search and to find His people, to draw them back to His table and to His heart by His love. In this special season, He is full of joy over those who are willing to recognize Him as the Father once again.

Can't You Rejoice with Me for Half an Hour?

God is standing before us. We may have been hurt by our Christian upbringing, by churches, pastors and all kinds of bad experiences, but He is pleading with us, almost like a beggar. In the Garden of Gethsemane, Jesus asked His disciples: **"Could men not keep watch with Me for one hour?" (Matthew 26:40).** Just like that, He is asking you right now, "Can't you rejoice with Me for half an hour or forty-five minutes in praise and worship?" We should be able to open our mouths and worship, without feeling like a hypocrite and without being convinced that this just does not suit our personalities. Should we not want to share God's joy about the abundance of life that is breaking forth everywhere? This might perhaps be a first step. Why do we not command the raging, despaired child that is still stomping its feet in us to hush? Then, we step out and say, "Okay, I will sing to my God. I will look to my God who is pleading to me

The Father of Compassion

with tears in His eyes: 'My child, can't you rejoice with Me for half an hour?'" We may not get healed, but it certainly is a good start—just joining with others to share God's joy. His joy will spill over into your life!

When I went to a conference with Vineyard founder John Wimber in the late 1980s with an injured knee, God led me to one of Wimber's team members. He quickly diagnosed the problem without engaging in any deep counseling or healing session. Then he said, "Come with me," and I just limped into the meeting with my hurting knee. During that meeting, some of God's glory spilled over into my life. I will never forget how my heart was overwhelmed with joy just because I was willing to come alongside with God, rejoicing together with Him over the things He was doing in other people's lives during that conference.

Curiosity is not prohibited as long as it is pure, and as long as you are watching, eager to share God's joy. Can you imagine what God is trying to convey by this amazing statement? "If just one person is getting saved, heaven is rejoicing; there is a celebration going on when this person's name is being written down in heaven" (see Luke 15:7). And while heaven is looking at the person and the angels are dancing, God stands before you, pleading, "I am asking you for these fifteen minutes, for this half-hour of praise. Would you give this time to Me and share My joy in spite of your contradicting emotions, your bitterness, and your resentments? Rejoice with Me, your Creator God!"

And maybe something in you will start changing. Maybe your heart will soften so the Holy Spirit can touch the deep and hidden areas of your soul, where unresolved issues and hurts are buried. Maybe He can start leading you out of the dungeon of the law. The law brings nothing but death. It **"was added"** (**Romans 5:20** ASV), like Paul said, and represents some kind of crutch or cast that God prescribed to His people. It was God's plan that the increase of sin would bring His people to a place where they were finally willing to surrender and learn that the works of the law and all the things we are able to do by ourselves will not save us.

The Eclipse of the Father

God may then reveal the inner images that are still eclipsing the reality of the Father in you. Many people derive their ideas of what a mother and a father are supposed to be like from the experiences with their own parents during their childhood years. These images can almost be like a solar eclipse, where the moon pushes itself in front of the sun. Like the moon darkens the sun, these borrowed father and mother images with their dim glow are blocking our view of the heavenly Father. The resulting darkness is so severe that even we as Christians have only a very shallow idea of who God really is.

You will not be able to break through until these solar bodies have been brought down, until the moon of your father and mother images lose their power over your life, and you start leaving these mental pictures behind. Doing this will also enable you to honor your parents in a new and different way.

Interestingly enough, our idealistic images can be more dangerous than the negative ones because they have an even greater power to keep us in bondage. We may continue to worship the moon instead of entering into the riches of our heavenly Father. The idealized images of our earthly fathers, as

The Father of Compassion

good as our experiences with them may have been, are still eclipsing the light, robbing us of the true Fatherhood that God wants to give us.

Only Jesus Can Reveal the Father to Us

Out of the deep feelings of lack, our soul is prone to project our desire to be fathered and mothered by Christian leaders, pastors, or mature, seasoned Christian women and mothers. This is normal; there is nothing wrong with it. God may use these people as crutches to help us bridge the gap. But Jesus clearly said, **"do not call anyone on earth 'father'!" (Matthew 23:9).** If we get too closely attached to these spiritual fathers and mothers, we are like children from broken, fatherless homes. They see another child's father and think, "I would like this man to be my father; that's how I imagine a father to be." These fathers will then become the objects of their dreams. Still these men will never be their real fathers, because they did not beget them. They will always remain fantasies.

The "Father of all fathers" is totally different from any earthly father we could ever experience during our lifetime. Jesus said, **"no one knows the Father except the Son and those to whom the Son chooses to reveal him" (Matthew 11:27).** Only Jesus can reveal the Father of all fatherhood to you—only Jesus. He is not just what your heart desires multiplied by ten, He is much more. The "Father of all fatherhood" can only be revealed to each one of us individually. Jesus said, **"If you really knew me, you would know my Father as well" (John 14:7).** We can learn to see the Father more and more in Jesus. As in a mirror, we are getting a revelation of who our heavenly Father really is.

Father

The Specific Hallmark of the Father

Our Father is love and His love has many different facets. The specific hallmark of the Father's love is compassion. He is the "Father of compassion" (see II Corinthians 1:3) who says, **"I will have mercy on whom I will have mercy, and I will have compassion on whom I will have compassion" (Exodus 33:19).** Compassion means that God loves us just the way we are, even if we are not very easy to love. Compassion is love that is poured out over whatever we despise and find disgusting, over things we deny and dissociate from, over areas of our lives that cause us to hate and to destroy ourselves by different means such as overeating or anorexia. Compassion pours out love over everything that seems despicable, even though there is no reason to do so. It is the outflow of the character of God, coming deep from His heart.

Compassion was God's spontaneous reaction to Noah's first sacrifice that he brought unto God after he had left the ark. And God promised, "Never again will I curse the ground because of man, even though every inclination of his heart is evil from childhood. And never again will I destroy all living creatures, as I have done. As long as the earth endures, seedtime and harvest, cold and heat, summer and winter, day and night will never cease" (see Genesis 8:21-22). And, a little later He added "I have set My rainbow in the clouds, and it will be the sign of the covenant between Me and the earth, showing that I am a Father of compassion who is reaching down from heaven with loving care" (see Genesis 9:13-15). Yes, He is indeed reaching down on everything that we ourselves hate and would like to spit out, expel, and push to the side.

The Father of Compassion

We do not even know what compassion is, although those of us who have children may feel a dim reflection of it in our hearts from time to time. It may rise within you after you spanked your child too hard or in a surge of anger, that suddenly you find yourself overwhelmed with compassion over your sobbing little one. One night a father came knocking on my door. He had been wandering aimlessly through the streets for hours like a lunatic. His eyes were full of terror because he had hit his child. He looked like a ghost. After his outburst, compassion had welled up inside of him over his child as he saw the bleeding in his face from the beating, and over the panic and sorrow he had caused—not only to this little one, but also to his brother who stood next to him and kept pleading. "Dad, please stop! It was me, it was me!" We do not really know what compassion is. Everything we know is only a shallow representation of the incredible compassion that God has for us. We just cannot imagine how God feels about us. We still believe deep in our hearts that He is condemning us and that He will brutally collect whatever we owe Him. We are unsure of what might happen to us once we get to meet Him.

We must understand why the "Father of compassion" has given **"all judgment to the Son?" (John 5:22)** He no longer judges! He neither keeps a stick or whip! The Father has given judgment to the Lamb that was slain in order to be fully available to us as the "Father of compassion," the God of all comfort. Do you actually believe that anything in this world could ever snatch you out of His hand? The Father surely will not let go of you, unless you choose to run away from Him; He is an abyss of compassion!

Father

The Heart of God Is Drawing Near to Us!

Throughout the Bible we can observe one thing—whenever people show the first sign of repentance, the heart of God draws near to them immediately. As soon as the people of Israel tore their clothes and put some ashes on their heads, the Father of compassion just melted and drew close to them.

Maybe we can compare it a little to those men who come home with a box of chocolates and roses to appease their wives and yet deep inside they know that sooner or later the same shortcoming will almost certainly happen again. But nevertheless their wives are overjoyed and blown away by this little sign of affection. They tend their roses, cut the stems, put them in water overnight to make them last longer, and they keep drawing close to the blossoms to soak in its fragrance. In the same way, God is moved by the few roses and the tears we offer to Him when we repent. Why do you think the Holy Spirit would rest on us? It is only because of God's compassion. He is stirred in His heart whenever we confess our sins and draw near to Him. Our meager repentance stimulates His compassion. He is the Father of compassion, the God of all comfort, your Father and my Father!

Whoever has tasted the compassion of our Father knows His heart: "You are no longer living under the law. There is no condemnation because I have extended My mercy on you! For no particular reason, I have decided to show you My compassion." Once this knowledge is instilled in our hearts, we may even be able to be compassionate with ourselves, and with our brothers and sisters as well. For this reason, Jesus kept telling us, **"Be merciful, just as your Father is merciful" (Luke 6:36)**. We are to be merciful in order to be sons and daughters of the merciful

The Father of Compassion

Father who causes His sun to rise on the evil and the good, and who **"is kind to the ungrateful and wicked" (Luke 6:35).**

The Compassion of Jesus

The mercy of God found a special expression in the life of Jesus, our Lord and Savior. He went to see a demon-possessed man in the region of the Gerasenes (see Mark 5:1-20) who was living in caves, bound with chains. The Father extended His mercy over this man and the powers of destruction fled immediately from God's gentle breath of compassion. So strong were these destructive powers that two thousand pigs were drowned in the lake. Another time, Jesus went into the arcades around the pool of Bethesda. Among hundreds of sick people, He found the one who said, "I don't have anybody to help me. I have been paralyzed for thirty-eight years." The passionate mercy of our God reached down upon the loneliness and abandonment of this man and found an expression in Jesus' simple words: "Get up! Pick up your mat and walk" (see John 5:8).

When Jesus hung on the cross, tortured and tormented, the same compassion reached out, even amidst the agony of His excruciating pain. Mustering all of His strength, He turned to the criminal who was hanging next to Him and said: **"Today you will be with me in paradise. Arm in arm, you and I will reach the realm of God's mercy in paradise" (Luke 23:43).** Maybe someone reading this feels so lost and left behind that he cannot even imagine that God especially loves to reach out to those on the margin, who feel out of place and unwanted.

Jesus never went to the healthy and righteous, but to the lost sheep of Israel in order to save that which was lost. He came to embrace the crying, stomping, and pounding children, those who feel so unloved that they kept rubbing their heads on their pillow until there was a bald, sore spot. Our Father of all comfort wants to take these children into His arms and touch them gently. He also wants to reassure the inner child in you, telling you, "My child, everything that belongs to Me is yours." God wants to put His stamp of approval on you and proclaim, "You are My desired one." He wants to affirm and approve your very existence and let you know that you were intended to be and there is a purpose to your life!

The Father Is Rejoicing Over You

Many people just fall through the cracks somehow. Their existence seems to be an accident, an error, something that was unplanned. They feel like they are without that stamp of approval. No one ever proclaimed "My desired one" over them; nor was there a father rejoicing when they came into being. But when God in His mercy reaches down to you, His tears and His tender mercy will soften your heart. He will cast a new foundation of His love in you and give you a new base to stand on in areas where you previously could not accept yourself where you kept denying the secrets of your life because they were just too painful to face. Maybe your father did not honor and affirm you; maybe he hurt or abused you. Yet the Father of compassion approves of you and gives you a firm foundation to rest on.

He rejoices over you with gladness, making it publicly known, "My Son, My daughter, today I have begotten you. You came into being because I wanted you to exist. You are not an accident, the result of two people losing control of themselves. You were not created by the will of a man or by the will of flesh.

The Father of Compassion

You were not created just because somebody wanted a son, an heir in the family, or someone to take over the family business. I, the Father of compassion, created you so I could rejoice over you forever and proclaim over you for all eternity: My daughter, My beloved daughter, you are the joy of My heart! My son, My dear son, I am proud of you! You are My child, noble and worthy."

Prayer

Father, I praise You. You are able to remove everything that is still eclipsing and darkening Your Fatherhood—everything that is shielding our hearts like a concrete slab, like a wall of brass, everything that keeps You hidden behind a heaven of brass and that makes us believe You are a distant judge. Thank You Lord that the red hot passion of Your mercy, the stream of Your comfort will melt these heavens of brass, crush the concrete slabs, overthrow idols of false fatherhood, and break the beating rod of the imaginary heavenly tyrant. The father and mother images that are still haunting or deceiving us, keeping us in bondage either through hate or through admiration will be washed away. You, the Father of compassion, will gently wrap Your hands around our clenched fists until we are able to let go of these destructive images, painful experiences, past hurts, and lay them down at the cross. We will then come to rest in Your secure anchorage for all eternity. Oh what an overwhelming treasure of mercies! Glory to You, glory to You, oh blessed God and Father of our Lord Jesus Christ, Father of compassion and God of all comfort.

Thank You, Holy Spirit, for staying close by as we are facing these dark places in our hearts; one single beam of the light of Your compassion pierces our loneliness like a laser beam, but not only that, it pierces our very mind, soul, and body as well. Once again, we want to give You our lives—spirit, soul, and body.

Father

We ask You, Holy Spirit, show us Jesus and in Him show us the Father. Point out the reality of the heaven of brass and lead us to the cross. As a mother comforts her child, comfort us, oh God. I bless you in the name of the Father God. I call down upon you His ardent compassion; may it "brood" over you and bring forth the new creation. I call down upon you the living hope so His plans for you may be accomplished. Amen!

ELEVEN

The Tender Love of the Father

The Character of the Holy Spirit and His Workings

Whenever we are talking about the Holy Spirit, we are talking about the love of God. The Spirit of God and His love are inseparable, for God is Spirit and God is love. He cannot be divided up. He is One. And since the Spirit and the love of God are indivisible, the New Testament keeps mentioning the fellowship of the Holy Spirit. This healing Power restores and reinvigorates relationships—be it in the context of small cell groups, a large congregation, the body of Christ as a whole, or even beyond.

The Holy Spirit and Love are Indivisible

Paul brought the Holy Spirit and love to a common denominator in a well-known verse: **"And hope does not disappoint us, because God has poured out His love into our hearts by the Holy Spirit, whom he has given us" (Romans 5:5).** Wherever the New Testament talks extensively about the Holy Spirit, there is also a special emphasis on love. For example, in John 14-17, Jesus mentioned the fact that He was going to give His life for His friends in order to honor the Father by total obedience to His perfect will. He also talked at length about the Holy Spirit, and in this respect made the following statement, **"If anyone loves me, he will obey my teaching. My Father will love him, and we will come to him and make our home with him" (John 14:23).**

The entire book of Acts, such a poignant testimony of the power and the fullness of the Holy Spirit, is another example and simply cannot be conceived of without the tangible love of God flowing through the church at Jerusalem. **"All the believers were one in heart and mind. No one claimed that any of his possessions was his own, but they shared everything they had" (Acts 4:32).**

Finally, think about the famous chapters 12 and 14 of I Corinthians that deal with the gifts of the Spirit. Paul is talking about the wealth of the gifts, talents, and callings that the Holy Spirit bestows on every single one of us, to help adorn and clothe the "bridal church" in shining white. These two chapters rest on the hinge of the legendary love hymn in I Corinthians 13 where Paul said:

> **"If I speak in the tongues of men and of angels, but have not love, I am only a resounding gong or a clanging cymbal.**
>
> **If I have the gift of prophecy and can fathom all mysteries and all knowledge, and if I have a faith that can move mountains, but have not love, I am nothing.**
>
> **If I give all I possess to the poor and surrender my body to the flames, but have not love, I gain nothing" (I Corinthians 13:1-3).**

The Tender Love of the Father

Paul concluded the chapter by emphasizing that **"tongues"** will be stilled, **"knowledge"** will pass away, **"prophecies"** will cease, but in the end a perfect thing will come and every transitory imperfect thing will be done away with. **"And now these three remain: faith, hope and love. But the greatest of these is love" (I Corinthians 13:13).**

The Holy Spirit Is a Person

Only human beings can love. No robot or stamp-collection will ever love you and neither will a computer, regardless of how detailed your knowledge of it may be. Even if you spend ten, twelve, or even fourteen hours a day working on it and it has become more intimate to you than your closest loved ones, it will never be able to love you. No impersonal object could ever return our affection. An animal may be capable of love to a certain extent, but it cannot love you in a spiritual sense.

We all know that only a person can truly love. The Holy Spirit is a Person. In the Holy Spirit we experience the fullness of the Godhead, as the Father and the Son come and make their home in us through Him (see John 14:23). As the Holy Spirit dwells in us, the Father and the Son saturate our existence with the fullness of life, with the fragrance of the love of the Father, and the love and friendship of the Son, our first-born Brother and Savior, Jesus Christ. The Holy Spirit, this third Person of the Godhead, is the love of the Father and the Son poured out into our hearts.

The Tender Love of God

We should give His love a try. Love in general has several different faces: The first one encompasses tenderness, gentleness, and kindheartedness, this indescribable, delicate mystery that can hardly be put into words. That is the flavor of the Holy Spirit. No human love, be it male or female, is as gentle, perceptive, dedicated, and utterly affectionate as the love of the Holy Spirit. Nothing compares to the Holy Spirit in His tenderness, meekness, and devotion.

The prophet Elijah experienced this kind of love. He feared that the Lord would react furiously, shaking the earth and throwing rocks through the air because he had run from Jezebel. However, God was not in the earthquake and He was not in the storm. Neither was He manifesting Himself in the fire this time. Yet there was a gentle whisper, a soft air current, an evening wind caressing his skin like a mild spring breeze, kissing him, murmuring around him, and gently stroking him. It was the kind of wind that is so pleasing to our faces that we close our eyes and turn our faces toward it. It was not possessive, but deeply affectionate and beautiful beyond description.

When Elijah heard this soft wind, he covered his face (see I Kings 19:13) because he knew it was the Lord. Read Song of Solomon and you will glimpse the tenderness and affection of the Holy Spirit. If you ever had an encounter with the love that the Father and the Son are pouring out through the Holy Spirit, you know something of the ecstasy, the overwhelming experience of being touched in your inmost being.

Paul experienced the love of God like few of us ever have. One time, he was allowed to cast a glance into the third heaven. This experience was so indescribably beautiful that God had to give Paul a **"thorn in my flesh" (II Corinthians 12:7)** to keep him from becoming conceited. Some people are able to recognize the Father's kiss, the touch of grace that God put into His very creation that we have often treated so lightly.

The Tender Love of the Father

The Fragrance of the Love of God in Us

On the Mediterranean Island of Sardine, I once discovered the gentle touch of God in the beauty of creation. We were camping in the dunes. They were covered over and over with beautiful white lilies that grew in the sand. The flowers were just perfect, with six stars and a circle of twelve star-shaped blossoms and six pistils in the middle. As we bowed down to get a closer look, there was an irresistible fragrance emanating from each flower. It was as sweet and pleasant as the fragrance of cinnamon. The only thing that comes close to their aroma is the scent of Daphne, which blossoms in winter, usually in January and sometimes in February in the mild sunlight. Even though the ground may still be frozen and covered with snow, Daphne spreads its entrancing perfume, so sweet and mild. It is absolutely charming, just like the love of God in which He courts us.

This helps us to understand why Paul talks about **"the fragrance of life" (see II Corinthians 2:15-16)** that is in the disciples of Jesus. The Holy Spirit in our hearts is oftentimes like a little plant, growing out of the barren sand dunes that are still dominating our lives. He spreads the fragrance of the precious presence of God. Women, men, and children who are living with God radiate with it because the Father planted the Holy Spirit into them, even though many issues remain in their lives that require healing and reclamation.

Have you ever sensed the fragrance of God's love in other people? It is just a privilege for us to spend time together and to discover each other in the body of Christ. There may be somebody standing in front of you at a conference who hardly dares to talk to you and all of a sudden you feel that precious scent of love in that person. She may feel like she is merely one of a thousand faces amidst an anonymous crowd, but the love of the Father and the Son is poured out into her heart and she is oozing with it.

This might be the reason why Christians, with all of the exuberant joy they experience, keep crying every once in a while—we realize how much God loves us, how dedicated, gentle, and utterly thoughtful He is. It is such a stunning realization that hits us over and over again. Every time during worship, tears start to well up inside of me because I am simply overcome by the tenderness of His love and by the beauty of who He is.

The "Craziness" of Love

This is my second point—genuine, true love is not only gentle, it is also intense and forceful. It can almost be crazy at times, willing to show the weirdest behavior, such as the things people do when they are madly in love and passion is burning inside of them. All too often, though, these wells of childlike spontaneity and playfulness get locked up when we enter into "wedlock." We become totally boring—just the average decent couple. Love is no longer crazy and passionate. The husband tends to let himself go at home and the only thing that still gets him excited is watching sports on television. If he ever happens to take her out, he will most likely choose his favorite hamburger place. No more adventure is involved.

Do we realize how much our spouses are longing for us to become crazy with love once again? A friend of mine is a huge example to me in this matter. When he was celebrating his fiftieth wedding anniversary, he put on his old wedding tuxedo. Of course, it needed a couple of alterations, buttons had to be moved, seams widened, and whatever else a clever tailor had to do to make it fit. But it just had to be the old suit! His wife put on her wedding gown; I had the bells rung for them, and they rode that horse carriage once again. These two "moss-grown" folks, with their hearing aids and other ailments had chosen to do something totally crazy! We need to understand something: Out of love, God does things that seem utterly crazy to us.

In the Old Testament, we read how God coped with His people, the Israelites. Many of His methods seemed to be mere craziness. Think of how God dealt with the prophets. Ezekiel was not allowed to leave through the door, but had to break a hole into one of the walls of his study in order to go in and out while he was in captivity in his parsonage (see Ezekiel 8:7-8).

Or remember Isaiah, a well-respected priest, an educated man with a keen mind who knew and loved his God, who had to go naked through the streets of his city. Think of Hosea, who had to marry a prostitute and have children with her in order to share a little bit of God's pain over His people cheating on Him. Hosea experienced a portion of God's agony. He had to live under the roof of the temple together with God's idolatrous people, who would come to the Lord on the Sabbath, but the day after, sleep around with their Baals and everyday idols (see Hosea 3:1).

Yet the craziest thing that God ever did was to become man— a man just like you and me. God loved us to a point where He became crazy enough to empty Himself and deliver Himself into the hands of the people He had been longing for and reaching out to in His crazy, incredible love. Love is powerful. Love is **"as strong as death,"** as Solomon sang (**Song of Solomon 8:6**). Love does extraordinary things that are sometimes difficult to comprehend.

Father

Out of love, people set out on paths not even knowing where they will end up. In God's relationship with us, we can experience this adventurous spirit of the power of love that gets ahold of us and at times knocks us over in an impetuous embrace. But this kind of love overcomes every fear and every reservation on our end. It releases a boldness and courage in us that we had never expected ourselves to be capable of. This is also a part of the work of the Holy Spirit.

Vulnerable Love

Now I want to cover my third point: Love can only be real if it is willing to be vulnerable. Whoever chooses to be self-protective in order to avoid being hurt cannot receive love and cannot give love himself. God is vulnerable; He made Himself vulnerable by entering into a covenant with the Hebrew people He led out of Egypt with His mighty hand—an eternal, irrevocable covenant. God made Himself vulnerable in the Person of Jesus of Nazareth, who wept over individuals and entire cities; His heart melted in compassion over the people that were like sheep without a shepherd. He was willing to let everybody approach Him, and the unbelief and hardness of heart He encountered frequently made Him angry. He delivered Himself into the hands of man—this **"King of the Jews" (Matthew 27:37)**—frail and deprived of all His power, except the power of love. **"Father, forgive them, for they do not know what they are doing!" (Luke 23:34).**

Love is always vulnerable and the most vulnerable side of God is the Holy Spirit. God made Himself utterly vulnerable by pouring out His Holy Spirit into our hearts. He is willing to dwell in us, amidst everything that is still in rebellion against Him, everything that wants to strike back, and everything that is hurting and revolting.

The Tender Love of the Father

We can compare the Holy Spirit in us to a child in a mother's womb. There is probably nothing more vulnerable than the unborn child inside of a woman. It is totally at the mercy of his mother. All of her thoughts and emotions, every hint of rejection and every fear is passed on to the child. She may even have the baby aborted without anybody ever taking notice of the child—"my womb, my choice." That is how vulnerable God has made Himself through the Holy Spirit. He has made His home in you and He feels everything you feel and suffers with you; He is moved by everything that moves you and everything that concerns you, whatever it may be.

You can grieve the Holy Spirit; you can stifle Him; but unless you leave Jesus, the Holy Spirit will stay in you. Do we understand why Jesus said, **"And everyone who speaks a word against the Son of Man will be forgiven, but anyone who blasphemes against the Holy Spirit will not be forgiven?" (Luke 12:10)** In other words, if we purposely abort the love of God, if we step on it, kick and ultimately trash it, we will cause indescribable pain to God's heart. Could we ever begin to fathom how privileged we are that the Father, the Son, and the Holy Spirit have come to make Their home with us through the Holy Spirit?

Something else becomes quite clear from this point of view: There is only one Spirit. Paul said in his letter to the Ephesians: **"There is one body and one Spirit..." (Ephesians 4:4).** There is not a different Holy Spirit for Charismatics, another one for Pentecostals, another one for Baptists, and yet another one for Catholics, or Episcopalians, each one tailored to the particular traditions and forms of worship that have evolved in the individual denominations. There is only one Spirit because there is only one God, one Father, and one Lord Jesus, because the love of God is indivisible. If you are a mother, it is your deepest desire to give yourself wholeheartedly to each one of your children. In the same way, it is the deepest longing of God to love all of His children with the same love—all of them!

We have not even begun to talk about the gifts of the Spirit, like the gift of prophecy or speaking and singing in tongues. I have not touched that subject because our focus is not on the gifts, but the person of the Holy Spirit. It is all about the love of God manifested in the Holy Spirit. We are all in desperate need of this love because we are created in the image of God and no human love could ever fill that void in us. No human being can ever give our spirit the fulfillment we desire—no woman, no man, no child, nobody! We are created in the image of God and no one else but Him can satisfy our deepest longing for love. When the Holy Spirit comes, the void in us is filled and we are able to live in relationships in a way we would have never imagined possible.

Satisfied By the Holy Spirit

I was in the service of the church for a long time and I really loved being a pastor. It is, however, a position where you are supposed to constantly love people, and that can be difficult when your own heart is not satisfied. If you are lacking this deep fulfillment in the Holy Spirit, the job of a pastor can become a heavy yoke, a burden that destroys your whole life. Nobody can endure this kind of pressure for an extended period of time. I remember the turning point in my own life. Everything changed when I opened my heart and my hands for the Father's love and said, "Holy Spirit, I welcome You into my life!" It was like somebody had turned on the light. God started to nourish me and to satisfy my heart, just like Jesus had promised, **"I am the bread of life. He who comes to me will never go hungry, and he who believes in Me will never be thirsty" (John 6:35).** If we eat and drink from the bread and the water of love, our lives become easy. Somehow your specific gravity changes and you are released to live.

From that time forward, my ministry was no longer toilsome because the mountains of ceaseless obligations that had been piling up in front of me were finally gone. No longer was I haunted by the constant fears of failure and the feeling that I would have to quit the ministry someday and flee to a place where nobody would know me. No longer did I have to wrestle down suicidal thoughts. The work of the ministry became feasible after all; I started enjoying it, even to the point where it became a great pleasure to me.

Heavy burdens were lifted off my marriage as well. Finally it was no longer the congregation that held the first priority, the second, even the third, followed by the youth group, the board of deacons, the prayer group, the mail, and so on and so on. When my wife and I took our weekly night off, something a dear brother had suggested to us, I was always totally drained. I had no energy left to engage in deeper conversation and my only thoughts circled around going to bed and finally getting some rest. The Holy Spirit wants to reinvigorate your life and put your marriage first once again, just as God has always intended it to be. Your congregation will then be second in line and no longer prone to suck the life out of you.

There is only one thing that will choke the fire of the Spirit in us and cause Him to withdraw—our pride and disobedience.

Father

The Holy Spirit and human pride and disobedience just do not go together well. The Holy Spirit is the Spirit of God's love and love means unreserved devotion. The Holy Spirit will always nudge you to dedicate yourself with all of your heart, mind, and strength. If you are led by the Spirit, He will cause you to turn to Him like a child asking, "Lord, what is next? Here I am, your child. Please fill me again, I need to be totally filled and satisfied by You. I want to be set on fire by Your love."

Throughout the history of our western culture, we have developed certain traditions that have kept us from yielding to the Holy Spirit. In fact, we have tried to impose limits on Him and to keep Him out of the church. We told Him what He was allowed to do in our midst. We put Him on a leash to the point where our spiritual lives were reduced to certain liturgical rituals. It should not surprise us that we sometimes have a long way to go, until our spirits, souls, and bodies are finally able to receive the outpouring of the Holy Spirit. Our hearts can be like an obstacle course. Because of the fear inside of us, it can take the Holy Spirit some time to reach the center of our being. Our fears can hinder us from really taking hold of our places as children. Nevertheless, the Holy Spirit is prepared for the challenge. The love of God overcomes all of these obstacles in our hearts.

God will take notice of every tiny step that we take, be it a little gesture like lifting our hands or kneeling down while we pray. He will come to meet us. God said, "If you know how to give good gifts to your children, how much more will I give you the Holy Spirit!" (see Luke 11:13). "I am so willing to hold you close and to touch you with the gentleness and the power of My love; I want to unleash the fullness of My life in you."

The Tender Love of the Father

Prayer

Father, from the depth of our hearts we ask You to forgive us for the many misconceptions we have of Your love, Your passionate longing for us, Your pain, and Your very heart. You want to be close to us and make Your home with us and love us, right in those very places where the smoldering wicks and the bruised reeds of our lives are located, the deep dungeons of our memories, the dark places of panic, terror and hurt, where we are unable to comprehend how much You love us. We may believe that Jesus died for our sins, but we still don't understand that You really intend to live with us, amidst all those unfinished and imperfect areas, in order to love on us and lift us up.

Father, from the depth of our hearts we ask You to forgive us our repeated misconceptions of the Holy Spirit. You, the Father, have given the deepest part of Your heart, Your Spirit, to Your beloved, bruised Son, the Exalted One, as a reward for His suffering so He could pour out this precious Spirit on all flesh, on sons and daughters, children and youth. Father, we simply didn't understand Your joy—the joy that causes all heavens to cheer because You decided to put Your innermost being, the most costly gift of Your heart into the pierced hands of Your Son. You knew that only Your Spirit would be able to restore our dignity.

We ask You Jesus, the Baptizer with the Holy Spirit, to please forgive us. We didn't understand what You were trying to tell us when You said, "It is good for you that I leave, for after I received the innermost being of My Father and your Father, I will come to stay forever in your hearts. I will stay in your hearts until the end of the world, until the day when we will see one another face-to-face. In the Person of the Holy Spirit, I will be with you at all times and nothing will be able to snatch you out of My hand because I will live in you.

147

Father

I will love you from the inside and make you strong and beautiful. I will put the fragrance of divine love deep inside of you and everything in you that is still crude, full of anger, unrefined, numb, harsh, cold, and easily irritated will be touched and transformed by My meekness and gentleness. Everything in you that still feels miserable, weak, and lacking will be impacted by My breath and My fire when I come to live within you with the power of this unfathomable love."

Father, we repent with all our hearts for the reservation we held against the precious gift of Your Holy Spirit. We ask Your forgiveness, where we didn't recognize You behind all the disguises that man and theology put around Your Holy Spirit—where some in prideful self-preoccupation considered the Holy Spirit their private property.

Father, please accept our plea for forgiveness. We ask You to cleanse us from all these false, distorted concepts; cleanse us from our fears; cleanse us where we have been hurt by people who abused Your Spirit; cleanse us with Your blood, wherever we grieved and choked You, where we rejected Your love and imposed limits on You. Forgive us for all those times when we were only looking for power and neglected Your gentleness, meekness, and humility. Would You please forgive us Lord?

We ask You to please forgive us for when Your Spirit was expelled from our churches, even on a national level, where we put limits and restrictions on Your overflowing love and intentionally put others and ourselves at risk to die of thirst and starvation from the trimmed-down gospel we preached.

Father, You are so gentle and full of tenderness that You keep asking us over and over again: Do you really want more? Do you really want Me to come with all of My love? Do you want Me to love you with My love, the love of the Creator of heaven and earth? May I

The Tender Love of the Father

love you with the energetic love of Jesus who gave Himself for you? May I also love you with the meekness and gentleness of a dove, a love that falls like dew on your innermost being—may I really do that?

Holy Spirit, You are this love of God that is poured out into our hearts and we ask You now, crying out like children: Come, oh love of the Father and of the Son, come to stay with us!

Father, we thank You for touching our hearts and giving us the key to life, to restored relationships, to Your anointing and healing. You have clothed us in robes of righteousness, embracing us and kissing us with the Father's kiss.

I praise You, Holy Spirit, for everything that You still have in store for us: We will drink from the water of life; we will be filled with the bread of the Father's love; we will sit at the Father's table and rise as His sent and commissioned ones. In fact, we will freely walk in and out of the Father's house in the glorious freedom of the sons and daughters of God. Amen.

TWELVE

The Father's Discipline

Refined by Fire

"**I**n your struggle against sin, you have not yet resisted to the point of shedding your blood.

And you have forgotten that word of encouragement that addresses you as sons [and daughters]: 'My son [my daughter], do not make light of the Lord's discipline [training], and do not lose heart when he rebukes [trains] you,

because the Lord disciplines [trains] those he loves, and he punishes everyone he accepts as a son.**"

"Endure hardship as discipline; God is treating you as sons [and daughters]. For what son is not disciplined [trained] by his father?**

If you are not disciplined (and everyone undergoes discipline), **then you are illegitimate children and not true sons** [and daughters].

Moreover, we have all had human fathers who disciplined [trained] us and we respected them for it.

How much more should we submit to the Father of our spirits and live!

Our fathers disciplined [trained] **us for a little while as they thought best; but God disciplines** [trains] **us for our good, that we may share in his holiness.**

No discipline seems pleasant at the time, but painful. Later on, however, it produces a harvest of righteousness and peace for those who have been trained by it (Hebrews 12:4-11).

When we deal with the Fatherhood of God, we automatically enter into the realm of the kingdom of God, for it is the joy and special pleasure of the Father to give His kingdom to His sons and daughters. That is what He takes pride in, what He is jealous for—that is His passion. Through Jesus, He said, "... **everything I have is yours" (Luke 15:31).** He designated us not only to become sons and daughters, but also heirs. He intends to let us share in what He has, even though He is God and does not need any help or counsel. He wants to include us in His plans and purposes, in His present-day creative dealings. Jesus pushed open the door of promise for us: "I have come from My Father and you may ask in My name. I am standing in front of My Father with My pierced body, looking into His eyes. Your prayers will reach the Father's heart because I am standing before the Father."

We, as Sons and Daughters, Are a Reflection of God's Majesty

Jesus said in the gospel of John, **"My Father...is greater than all" (John 10:29).** And since our **"Father...is greater than all,"** we as His sons and daughters will reflect something of

The Father's Discipline

His majesty. Whenever we pray, we are acting as representatives of a great Father and our thoughts, feelings, and actions will be inspired by Him. When David fought Goliath, he did not just send a quick prayer to heaven, such as "God, help me now!" He faced the giant, that monster of a man, as a representative of God and declared, "**...I come against you in the name of the Lord Almighty, the God of the armies of Israel, whom you have defied. This day the Lord will hand you over to me, and I'll strike you down and cut off your head. Today I will give the carcasses of the Philistine army to the birds of the air and the beasts of the earth, and the whole world will know that there is a God in Israel" (I Samuel 17:45-46).**

When the first Christians prayed for the persecuted apostles, they approached God Himself, the Creator of heaven and earth, who fills the earth and the sea with His glory. We do not serve a God of bare necessities, who is hardly able to get us through, and who can only help us to scarcely survive. Our God is the Creator of heaven and earth, the "Father of all Fatherhood," the God of all generations. Our God created the nations and ethnic groups of the earth. He keeps creating new things all the time, and scientists will never be able to fully explore everything that He in His infinite majesty and wisdom has called into being. That's our God, our Father!

The more we grow in our identity as sons and daughters of God, the more we develop an understanding of who this Father is, and the better we will comprehend what Paul meant when he said, "**... let your conduct be worthy of the gospel of Christ...**" **(Philippians 1:27 NKJV).** As sons and daughters, we represent God, not a certain denomination or church. We are not going out into the streets to deliver propaganda for a church, an association, or a certain group; we are the representatives of the awesome God, the Creator of heaven and earth. That makes all the difference! You are bearing His name and are representing Him, the awesome King. In Revelation, we can read in the letter to the church of Philadelphia that a time is coming when Jesus will give each one of us a new name: **"Him who overcomes I will make a pillar in the temple of my God. Never again will he leave it. I will write on him the name of my God and the name of the city of my God, the new Jerusalem, which is coming down out of heaven from my God; and I will also write on him my new name"** (Revelation 3:12).

We are like diplomats in the service of God. That reminds me of Mahesh Chavda, who comes from an Indian family living in Africa. Today, he resides in the United States. Together with his wife Bonnie, they have a tremendous healing ministry. They are also prayer watchmen standing "on the wall" every Friday night for their God, wherever they are. Through Mahesh, God has even raised dead people to life. You should see this man! Mahesh really is a diplomat in God's service. He ministers in an immaculate, double-breasted suit with tie because he is aware of his status, serving in the diplomatic corps of the awesome Almighty God, the Creator of heaven and earth. If large companies make their workforce dress neatly with suit and tie, how much more should the representatives of God be dressed in dignity, not by means of outward attire, but through our poise and what we are as children of a God who lives in us and transforms us?

Jews and Christians—an Alternative Society

As Christians, we represent an alternative society. God spoke clearly to His firstborn people (and this prophetically includes all the Jews and Gentiles): "**... be holy, because I am holy**" (**Leviticus 11:45**). This demand still haunts the Jewish people to this day. It is the actual reason for the anti-Semitism that flares up again and again because these people are set apart from everybody else. Hitler sensed this uniqueness and knew that they would ultimately not be subject to anybody. These people are paying their taxes—they serve in armies and make fabulous contributions to science, various professions, and the monetary business. However, you will never gain their ultimate allegiance because deep inside they know that God has set them apart. There is something alive in them that makes them utterly different, which convinced Hitler that this race needed to be eradicated. He was looking for a race that was willing to submit and be obedient to him.

Christians are a people who cannot be subjugated and will not bow to any worldly authority, but only to Jesus Christ. In North Korea, there is a statue of the last dictator that is one hundred or more feet high. It is a custom for people to bow before that image and lay down flowers at its feet. I once met a young couple who had made a resolution at the foot of this statue: "We will not bow. We belong to a people who do not bow down and compromise anymore."

"Ecclesia" (which translates into "the church" from Greek) means the fellowship of those who have been called out. You can tell who the Christians are. They do not go into hiding. They are not an integral part of society anymore. They share in this world by serving and regarding everybody else higher than themselves. They respect not only those who are born again, but sinners as well. They are distinctly different from the rest of society because God called them out and transformed them into His image. We carry Christ in us and He takes form in us.

Father

Not "In" but "Different"

Jesus says, **"If the world hates you, keep in mind that it hated me first" (John 15:18).** Once you are different from everybody else, you are "out." The highest objective in this world is to be "in" and to avoid standing out as being awkward because it hinders your own little success story. As a Christian you are no longer "in," you are different. Jesus Himself was different. He was even different from the way the religious people had conceptualized Him. Consequently, they crucified Him, but not before He called out a people for Himself and led them into the freedom of the sons and daughters of God.

This freedom is not a carte blanche for an immoral lifestyle, or a license to neglect our responsibility towards society and our nation. On the contrary! Out of all people, Christians ought to be the most loyal servants, as long as they are not deserting their ultimate allegiance to God. But the fact that we are different will cause us to get in trouble and stir up opposition and hatred toward us. There is a conflict between the powers of light and the powers of darkness. Jesus announced the coming kingdom of God, saying, **"The time is fulfilled, and the kingdom of God is at hand; repent and believe in the gospel" (Mark 1:15 NAS).** The kingdom of God overcomes everything; it is expanding in all the nations of the world and nothing can stop it.

Think about China. An incredible growth is taking place in China in the underground churches, but also in the official, registered churches. They keep growing and growing and millions upon millions are coming into the kingdom. Chinese Christians are preparing to go into Tibet. True disciples, men and women are sowing the explosive force of the gospel into ethnic groups and the systems of the world. Do not think that communism crumbled by accident. It was the explosive power of the kingdom of God, men and women giving themselves as living sacrifices to God which brought down communism. On the sacrifices of these devoted sons and daughters, God built His kingdom and destroyed the kingdom of communism.

Sons and Daughters Being Taught and Raised Up

The kingdom of God is being sowed and is gaining a foothold wherever sons and daughters represent their God. We need to give God room to teach us and raise us up to become mature sons and daughters. He wants to train us, His little ones whom He is taking by the hands, swinging us high up in the air, the ones He loves to play with and later hold close, covering us, forgiving our sins, and pouring out His mercy over us. But if someone is being raised up, there is also some pushing involved. God has His ways to get us out of our comfort zones. After all, we are destined to represent and model our God to the world.

It is a great privilege for us to be convicted of our sins by the Holy Spirit because it helps us to grow into a deeper awareness of God's holiness. It is not about one, big cleanup that takes care of the bulk of our old garbage. We will not be able to just move on after our conversion, thinking, "Well, that has been taken care of!" We have not even begun to understand what sin is. David was confronted with that fact, and he cried out: "Against You, You alone, have I sinned and done what is evil in Your sight, even before every human being that I have hurt by my sin" (see Psalm 51:4).

To Hate Sin

God is the One who is being hurt the most. If we could only imagine how we are hurting Him. He so generously offers us everything—the abundance of creation, the privilege of being called His sons and daughters, the riches of His gifts, His very heart, and the highly favored position He has granted us: "You are My sons and daughters who will reclaim My rightful property on this earth." We are deliberately and heedlessly hurting our God. It is completely inconceivable! If we allowed the Holy Spirit to convict us of this sin, there would be a rude awakening. We would weep and wail over the condition of our hearts and hatred toward sin would be permanently instilled in us. We can reach a point where playing with fire just does not seem appealing anymore. The desire to sin can actually be expelled from our lives forever. Jesus broke the power of sin over our lives on the cross. We do not expect the Holy Spirit to only bless and refresh us. We welcome Him as the Spirit of truth who reveals our sin to us and who leads us into a process of sanctification, so the holiness of God can take form in us.

Each one of us is radiating with the character of Jesus. The world will very well notice that in you. If Jesus is the main focus of your life, something will transmit from you and the people around you will not get entangled in it and fall, but they will see a reflection of Jesus in you. People will say, "There is something special about you. I wonder what it is? Tell me what is so different about you?" The process of sanctification that transforms each one of us into a reflection of Jesus is something totally mind-boggling. It is the main focus of God's training and discipline. This process of maturing includes God keeping obstacles in our way. Sometimes He will even let us walk all by ourselves for certain periods of time, because He wants us to grow up and make our own experiences.

God is a Father, but He comforts us like a mother comforts her child. Sometimes it is hard to conceive how patient He is.

The Father's Discipline

We can always come to Him with our bleeding knees and tell Him, "I blew it again, would You please forgive me?" And the Father will say, "Get up, son! Continue on your assigned path! Try again, because I am with you. I am greater than everything else and I am standing by you." It is our prayer that the Holy Spirit will not only touch individuals; we hope for entire cities to be affected and for repentance to break out all over the place. The church has to start realizing that we, as the people of God, have been called out to represent the holiness of God in the world. It is a huge heritage and a tremendous privilege that God is bestowing upon us when He says: "You shall become a reflection of Me!"

The Unorthodox Training Methods of God

Because we have to learn to embrace holiness as sons and daughters of God, He cannot always use a gentle hand to train us up. Sometimes He will make use of more drastic measures and He may even give us a good, solid spanking.

I still remember one of those occasions. I careened my car off the road and drove down a steep shoulder. The car turned over twice and landed on its roof. The roof was flattened and literally touched the steering wheel. Much later, when I was waking up out of my state of unconsciousness, I remembered seeing stars above me while the car was turning over. I also recalled what I was thinking: "The Father, the Father! This is not meant to be punishment, it is discipline. It's Him; He is teaching me a lesson. He is flattening the roof to block the steering wheel. He is teaching me not to steer my life all by myself anymore." How sobering it was when a farmer came to visit me in the hospital three days later, asking me if I would be willing to give him the rear axle of my nice car that I had been so proud of because his beat-up trailer could use a new one. These are God's training methods! God loves taking care of several issues at a time. He disciplined me while providing this dear farmer with a new axle.

I am so thrilled with God's ways of training us. Do you not love to graduate from one grade to the next in God's school? What a joy it is for a young man to realize that the compulsive drive to live out his sexual desires in an unwholesome way is suddenly gone. When we allow God to successively work on our hearts, we will experience sudden breakthroughs. What a privilege these training processes of God are.

Continue on, Jesus!

There is nothing more awesome than to see people in whom Jesus lives. I will never get enough of it. Whenever I see an elderly person who lives with Jesus, I feel so honored. What a treat it is to observe young people, who are still going through the rebellious times of their puberty, but they are already radiating with Jesus to some degree. There is something of Jesus being transmitted. God is the perfecter of our faith and He will reach His goal with us. God is persistent and totally committed, just as Jesus is, and He will not let go of us. But we have to give Him permission to train and discipline us by telling Him, "Continue on, Jesus! Stay at it! Come and move again in my life!"

We are God's voice in this world. Jesus made the challenging statement, **"He who hears you, hears Me…"** (Luke 10:16 NKJV). God entrusts us, His sons and daughters, with the things that are most urgent to Him. At the same time, God is generous. He said that we would be rewarded for everything we have done for Him. This is not meant to be some kind of payment; He simply wants to bring joy to us. Our God is building us up; He

The Father's Discipline

is the God of life and abundance. He wants us to enter into His fullness. However, we will only be able to enter into it, if we, as His sons and daughters are in obedience to His will. The wisdom of God is as high above our own human wisdom as heaven is above the earth. His ways are higher than our ways. Often, we are unable to see the full picture of why He, in His wisdom, is leading us in a certain direction.

God, What's Your Strategy This Time?

God's wisdom is immeasurably beyond our own and His ways are always different from ours. As sons and daughters, we are being trained to discern the often subtle hints of the Holy Spirit in order to understand how God wants us to proceed in a certain situation. Just look at the things that are reported in the Bible: God never does the same thing twice. He always chooses to do things differently the next time around. One time, He took five loaves of bread and two fish to feed five thousand people (see Matthew 14:18-20). On a similar occasion, there were only four thousand people to feed. Jesus could have reasoned, "Four loaves of bread should be plenty enough!" However, there were seven loaves of bread, and He decided to take all of them— even though this time there was more bread to begin with, they ended up having fewer baskets of leftovers! (see Matthew 5:35-39) God will always act differently from what He did at previous times.

Once, David was told to lead a frontal attack. Another time, David asked his God, whom he knew intimately, "God, what is Your strategy this time?" And God told him, "Look at the trees. As soon as the leaves start rustling, you shall attack from behind!" (see II Samuel 5:23-25) It is one thing to lead a frontal assault, but to wait until some leaves start moving must be some-what different for a great military leader like David. What God was saying to David might have sounded like, "Just marvel at the landscape—that will divert you. Then you may come from behind!" They won a glorious victory. God will always take a different route. But He needs sons and daughters who are absolutely trustworthy. To understand that He will not do it the same way twice, we need to know our God intimately. Every time we have to ask Him, "God we did it a certain way back then. How do you want us to move this time?" God will test us in this regard and He is raising up people who are wholly devoted to Him. He did the same thing with David's friends. They were absolutely loyal. Only for this reason, David was able to conquer the kingdom with them—first at Hebron and later at Jerusalem in Judea.

God Needs to Be Able to Trust Us

Jesus was absolutely trustworthy. In Revelation 19:11, He is called **"Faithful and True."** God could trust His Son with everything. When Jesus prayed, "Father, not My will but Yours be done," the Son was saying, "Father, You can absolutely trust Me! I will do whatever You want" (see Luke 22:39-46). God will keep training us, testing us, and building us up. God will use us to do unusual things. He may take us to places we would have never chosen ourselves. Prisons can be places that God uses, but who would ever go there unless he had to? Paul was a Roman citizen and in the prison at Philippi he started the first prison ministry on European soil (see Acts 16:23-34). The prison was shaken and the overseer came to the Lord. We need to yield our hearts even to the most peculiar ways of God.

As Christians, we have a particular standpoint with regard to the ways of God. His ways are holy and we are not always able to understand them. Sometimes we may be led in certain directions that require total dedication to God. God uses those ways for His kingdom. What would have happened if Jesus had not given His life on the cross? It would not have altered the fact that He had healed thousands, that He had multiplied bread, and walked on water. He would have been considered a wise man and a prophet who left us a great number of uplifting quotes to put on calendars. However, there would have been no redemption. In the same way, we need men and women who are willing to yield to the ways of God.

Martyrs for our God will stand very close to the throne of God. They will reign with Jesus for a thousand years. Can you imagine what it will be like to reign with Jesus? I personally believe in a coming millennium (see Revelation 20:1-7), because to me the Bible is the Word of God and thus is binding. I am convinced that God will show the nations of the world what true government can look like, after the people are no longer deceived by Satan. God will pour out His mercy once again.

The last words of Johann Christoph Blumhardt, a Lutheran pastor from the nineteenth century were, "God, open Your hands in compassion over the nations of the world!" This is also the cry of my heart. May God release His mercy over the nations! But how can His mercy and compassion even reach the nations, unless His sons and daughters are willing to be called out and dedicated to walk in the ways of their Father? Isaiah 6:8 says, "**...Whom shall I send? And who will go for us?**" For the prophet Isaiah, this included walking the streets of his city naked for an extended period of time. How weird! Does a priest not usually wear a different outfit?

Incorruptible Flesh

God is looking for people who are trustworthy and devoted. Bob Jones, one of my prophetic friends, used the expression

Father

"incorruptible flesh." With this term, he was trying to describe individuals who are straightforward and unwilling to deviate from the will of God. I want to plead with the young generation for a moment: Please take to heart what was going on in the story of the young prophet in I Kings 13. He had been commissioned by God to go to Bethel, the capital of the idolatrous northern kingdom of Israel, to deliver a message to King Jeroboam and to proclaim a prophetic sign—the grand, national altar would burst in the middle and the ashes on it would be scattered.

And that is exactly what happened. Jeroboam, who was about to bring a sacrifice, extended his hand and shouted, "Arrest him!" Immediately, his arm became stiff and he was unable to draw his hand back. Still standing on the steps of the altar, he begged the prophet: "Please, appease your God!" The young prophet prayed for the king and he was able to move his arm again. What happened here? I believe this is a prophetic hint to the fact that God wants to use young people in a mighty way, as inexperienced as they may be, because they have "incorruptible flesh," or to put it in other words, because they are fully devoted to God. They walk in total obedience and do not want any applause for themselves.

But what happened later in the account? God had clearly told the young prophet: "You shall not eat and drink there. Don't even sit down to talk (about the miracle that happened). They might even end up awarding you a medal of honor. You shall return home as quickly as possible, using a different road from the one that you took getting there. This way they will not be able to find you." However, there was an old prophet living in the city, who was already a little depleted and who kept talking about the good old days, when miracles still happened. When his sons came back home, they told him what the young prophet had done. He was gripped with such a longing that he just had to meet the young man. He rushed after him and said, "An angel appeared to me, telling me that you needed to come back with me and stay for dinner in my house." The young man fell for this trick and accepted his invitation. While they were eating, the Spirit of God came upon the old prophet and he prophesied over the young prophet that a lion would kill him on his way home because he had not been obedient to the word of the Lord. Imagine the tragic circumstances! Only a little while later, people found him dead indeed, with his donkey and the lion standing still next to him.

I am pleading with all of you, but I am especially concerned with the young people: Whenever God commissions you, there is only one adequate response. Do not look to the right or to the left. Do not pay attention to what people are saying or doing. Do what God is calling you to do and then step down into the ranks as quickly as possible to become invisible to men once again. We are executing the will and the directives of God; thus we should not receive honor for ourselves. God is looking for people who are willing to resist the admiration of men and refuse to talk about and spread the things they have done, people who just leave and head home on a different road. Our hearts need to be sanctified for the truth in order for us to become reliable sons and daughters who God can count on.

No Fear of Rejection, Pain, and Death

Paul said to the Corinthians, **"Do you not know that we will judge angels? How much more the things of this life!" (I Corinthians 6:3).** Just imagine, one day we will judge angels! What a high calling the sons and daughters of God have! Part of our glorious freedom is the fact that we are beyond the point of death. People are bound by their fear of pain and death. However, we, as sons and daughters of God, are advancing into a place of freedom where pain and death do not intimidate us anymore. We are able to declare, **"If we live, we live to the Lord; and if we die, we die to the Lord. So, whether we live or die, we belong to the Lord" (Romans 14:8).** That is a new level of freedom! Only when you are free from the fear of death are you really free. Only when you are free from the fear of pain and suffering are you really free. Anything less cannot be called true freedom.

We are proclaiming a false gospel if we tell Christians that they will not have to suffer in their walk with Jesus. There is a pill and antibiotic for every little ailment, so the gospel degenerates into a drugstore, granting us a life free of pain. But in reality, we have the most awesome freedom known to man. We are free from the need to curry favor with men, free from the fear of death, and free from the fear of pain.

We do not have to avoid pain at any cost. We are men and women who know that they have eternal life. It is already in us, in you and in me! We are no longer begging for a few more days, or a couple more years because we already have eternal life today. If we beg it is only for one thing: "Please, Lord, give us a little more time to bring in more fruit and possibly even see the day of Your return! Let me be here when You bring the harvest in, and when Your people rise up in power! I desire to be around when Your people will be a testimony of unity, mutual respect, and love. I want to see the day when Messianic Jews and the people of the nations will be dancing together, worshiping You, oh God!"

The Father's Discipline

Jesus, the carpenter's son, stood before the Roman governor unyieldingly. He did not beg for His life to be spared, but boldly proclaimed, **"You would have no power over me if it were not given to you from above ... "** (John 19:11). From that moment on, Jesus refused to talk to Pilate. Jesus was the Son of God and we are His brothers and sisters. We will grow to become mature, authentic, and noble in our poise. We will take our stand, full of confidence, walking in the freedom of the sons and daughters of God.

"Incredibly Happy, Absolutely Fearless, and Always in Trouble."

I would like to remind you of what the Quakers used to say: "Christians are incredibly happy, absolutely fearless, and always in trouble." There is no greater happiness than the kind that comes out of suffering. One of the best wines available is made from grapes which have been exposed to frost. The vinedresser holds off harvesting until the grapes have been exposed to freezing temperatures for one night and then they are picked and pressed. There is very little juice left in these grapes, but they are sweet and full of flavor. This is the taste of happiness that evolves from times of rejection, from the deep valleys of life in-between the high places. A deep sense of happiness comes from the knowledge that we are in Jesus, close to Him, and always on His side.

Once, our ministry came under attack on Swiss national television. We were publicly badmouthed and accused. I did not watch television that night, but I went on a long walk in the woods and fields. It was a glorious, moonlit night and God put that old hymn by Paul Gerhardt into my heart:

Father

My heart for joy is springing
And can no more be sad,
'Tis full of mirth and singing,
Sees naught but sunshine glad
The Sun that cheers my spirit
Is Jesus Christ, my King;
That which I shall inherit
Makes me rejoice and sing.

I walked through the night singing. I had not had such sweet moments with the Lord for a long time. My heart was filled with a deep supernatural sense of gladness that has not left me since. It just stayed with me as the underlying tune of my life. There is no greater happiness than the one that is found in the midst of suffering.

In the letter to the Philippians, which Paul wrote while he was imprisoned, he says over and over again: **"Rejoice in the Lord always. I will say it again: Rejoice!" (Philippians 4:4).** This is the most profound sense of joy you can ever find. We do not want to glorify suffering. If you are in the midst of it, we want to lay hands on you, believing with you for signs and wonders of restoration. And yet, God's ways are often different from our ways.

One day, I was talking to a blind young woman. She was sure that she would have never come to Christ if her eyes had not been blind. The fact that her natural eyes were closed caused the eyes of her heart to be opened. These were God's ways with her. God builds His kingdom even through people in wheelchairs. His kingdom is not only advanced through the strong and healthy, but also through the maimed and mutilated. I do not know why it has to be like that; God's ways simply surpass our understanding. God is at work, expanding His kingdom in many different ways in order to reach people everywhere. If God was willing to pay such a high price that He gave His Son on the cross for us to be saved—what does that tell us about the value that every single one of us has in His eyes? As the Quakers said: "Christians are incredibly happy, absolutely fearless, and always in trouble!"

Prayer

Father, thank You for being this awesome Father to us, who is drawing His children close to His heart. Sometimes You are simply spoiling us; You rejoice in us and comfort us like a mother would. You hold us tight and whisper, "Nobody will snatch you out of My hand!" At the same time, there is a passion in You for us to become real, to become men and women, sons and daughters who are willing to take a stand for You. You want to see us mature and join the army of God's people who are carrying the banner of the Lamb; an army who is not fighting with the weapons of flesh, but with the weapons of the Spirit; people who are ready to be sent out like lambs and sheep into a world filled with a wolf-spirit.

His army is advancing in the power and authority of God. They may walk through deserts, yet they will not perish. They may go through the fire, yet they are not burnt. They may be thrown into lions' dens, yet You, God, will close up the lions' mouths. They may be tossed into fiery furnaces, but You will send your angels to protect them. And if You don't send Your angels and we are being burned, we know that the smoke of our devotion is rising to Your throne and will unleash a harvest that surpasses anything we could ever imagine.

THIRTEEN

The Eternal Father
His Apostolic Church

In His high priestly prayer, Jesus addressed His beloved Father as "**...Holy Father**" **(John 17:11)** in order to affirm His willingness to submit to the holiness of God's ways. We are not only children of the Father, living in total dependence on Him; we are also maturing in our role as His sons and daughters. As sons and daughters, we are commissioned to represent the Father in this world. For this reason, Jesus said we are to be holy as our Father is holy, which means that we are to reflect His character.

The ABC's of Living in the Spirit

I should not even have to mention that for Christians, forgiveness is not an option. We have no choice, because He has forgiven us and His Spirit in us will forgive everyone who has harmed us. Even if we do not feel like forgiving and our soul is running rampant, we still forgive in the name of Jesus. In the same way, we have no choice but to release our hurts into the wounded hands of Jesus. Our hurts do not belong in our own hands. We are not to carry them around with us so as to beg for the pity of others. Our identity is not in our pain because Jesus took our wounds upon Himself.

One day, I was called to a church for an emergency intervention. These people told me, "We cannot deal with each other any longer because our hurts are already running too deeply." Brothers and sisters, how can we even talk like that under the cross of Christ? Somebody hung on that cross for every one of us. Though He was without sin, He was willing to be made sin and to become a curse for us.

Let us not allow ourselves to become so hung up on our hurts that we lose sight of the overwhelming sacrifice of Jesus. Our wounds and our pain belong to God. Only by placing our hurts into His hands will we experience what it means to **"bear one another's burdens…" (Galatians 6:2 NKJV)**. Whatever may be broken in the body of Christ will only be mended if we help each other carry our burdens. We are representing God, who is full of mercy and compassion. For this reason, we too have to be full of kindness, willing to release each other and to be reconciled to one another.

Advancing with the Vision of the Kingdom of God

At the same time, our heavenly Father is challenging us as His sons and daughters. He will not always pamper and coddle us. Instead, He wants us to grow as His sons and daughters. We are supposed to become strong and to advance with a mature vision of His kingdom.

God started out by calling Abraham, an old man, out of his retirement and sending him to a land he did not know. He declared: "If you will go, I will make you into a great nation and through you all the nations of the earth will be blessed" (see Genesis 12:1-3). When this old man had a child, God told him, "Give Me that child" (see Genesis 22). After the test was over, God renewed His promise to Abraham: "Because you didn't withhold your son, I will bless you, and in your name all the peoples of the earth shall be blessed."

Our God will not hesitate to throw the nestlings out of the nest when their time has come; He will nudge us out of our comfort zones. We are allowed to make mistakes, to fall, to have a bad day, and to mess up. However, He will always rejoice when He sees us boldly step out in His name. He will never accuse us. Trying to make the most out of one's talents has everything to do with boldness and audacity. Sometimes that will involve going beyond our limits and getting things wrong. Even then, God still appreciates our boldness. It is okay even for churches to make mistakes—this is how we get to know the Father's heart, learn to forgive one another, and remain dependent upon God.

The prophet Isaiah described our God like this: **"For a child will be born to us, a son will be given to us; and the government will rest on His shoulders; and His name will be called Wonderful Counselor, Mighty God, Eternal Father, Prince of Peace. There will be no end to the increase of His government or of peace, on the throne of David and over his kingdom, to establish it and to uphold it with justice and righteousness from then on and forevermore. The zeal of the Lord of hosts will accomplish this"** (Isaiah 9:6-7 NAS).

I especially like the name **"Eternal Father."** It means that our Father will never stop being Father. He will not take on a different role once the new heaven and the new earth replace the present ones. He will forever be our Father, the **"Eternal**

Father." In the same way, He does not just have a little love to give, He is love! God doesn't merely take on the role of a Father while we are immature children on this planet, He will keep His status forever. It's His character to be Father.

The Father Turned Over Judgment to the Son

He will remain the **"Eternal Father"** even after that great turning point, when books will be opened and the nations of the earth as well as every single one of us will be standing before the throne to give account. As a sign of His eternal Fatherhood, He turned over all judgment to His Son (see John 5:22). Otherwise, He would no longer be perceived as the Father, but the Judge that causes everyone to tremble. For this reason, the Father decided to turn over judgment to His Son. The Son, not the Father, will be the Judge—the Lamb that is standing in front of the throne, looking as if it had been slain (see Revelation 5:6).

The Father has given judgment over to His Son who, in His pierced body, will judge the world. Only One is worthy to break the seals and to pronounce judgment: the Lamb of God. That should reassure those of us who are still struggling with a distorted, tyrannical conscience and with false, gruesome ideas of how God is. He is our Father, our **"Eternal Father."**

God's Burning Desire for His People

Even in the midst of judgment, God will always remain our Father, the **"Eternal Father."** He has only one desire—to dwell among His people. In the book of Revelation, we read: "… **Now the dwelling of God is with men, and he will live with them…**" **(Revelation 21:3).** It is His deepest longing to be able to live among His children. Throughout the Scriptures, God revealed the sincere passion of His heart, the heart of a loving God. Out of all metaphors, He used a marriage to depict His relationship with His people. What an illustration!

Marriage is full of passion, of raw emotions, of ups and downs. He said to His people, **"I will betroth you to me forever; I will betroth you in righteousness and justice, in love and compassion" (Hosea 2:19).** God has made a covenant with His people. He did not have a few religious rituals in mind with the intention of straightening us out a little. He is not primarily interested in us understanding bits and fractions of Him in order to reflect Him dimly. He burns with passion for His people, for His elected ones. **"I will betroth you to Me for ever."**

God is not ashamed to say that He is a jealous God. Have you ever heard of any other God who said, **"... I the Lord your God, am a jealous God" (Exodus 20:5)** Can you imagine Buddha being jealous, or Allah, or all those Vishnus? The Living God, Creator of the universe declares, "I am a jealous God!" This is not a religious phrase or a theological formula, it is the truth. We need to read in Hosea where God said, "I have engaged Myself to you for eternity, but you are unfaithful to Me. I will lie in wait for her on the roadside to block your path because something in Me is wounded, because I am longing for your love. But you are betraying Me with other gods" (see Hosea 1 and 2).

Can you imagine a God who is almost begging for our love? In the person of Jesus, this God is standing in front of Peter, asking him: "Do you love Me? Do you love Me more than these?" (see John 21:15-17). Can you imagine that God does not even mind making Himself vulnerable? He is willing to come and ask you, "Do you love Me?" as if He depended on our love. He is a God who is not ashamed to let us know, "I am thirsty. Would you give Me something to drink?" (see John 4:7).

He is a God who desired His disciples to be close to Him in Gethsemane, uttering, **"My soul is overwhelmed with sorrow to the point of death. Stay here and keep watch with me"** (**Matthew 26:38**). He is a God full of passion, coming as a Bridegroom to summon His bride. Once, when Jesus was eating and drinking with His disciples, He defended them against the Pharisees who were accusing them for neglecting the proper days of fasting. He said: **"Can the friends of the bridegroom fast while the bridegroom is with them?"** (**Mark 2:18-20**, NKJV).

The Bride of Jesus Is Being Prepared in the Father's Heart

While we were in Jerusalem a couple of years ago, we stayed in a little apartment on the outskirts of the city. Right across from us, we could see the Mount of Olives. During the night, I had to look frequently over to that hillside. I knew that one day the feet of Jesus would touch that hill again because He promised it in Acts 1:11. What a hope we have! The Bridegroom will actually come, and we, His bride, will go out to meet Him. Paul said in I Thessalonians 4:18, **"Comfort one another with these words"** (NKJV).

Let us start pondering on this bride once again! It is a paradox that at the same time she is here on earth, in heaven the Father is working on her to prepare her. One day she will come down from heaven—just like the Ark of the Covenant, the Tabernacle, the Temple, just like Jesus Himself. They were all created in heaven first and later became visible on earth—just like the real Ark of the Covenant, the real Tabernacle, the real Temple, and the Son of Man. The real bride, although present here on earth, is already being adorned in heaven. She is being prepared in the Father's heart. Eventually, she will be revealed here on earth in her full glory.

Apostles of the Lamb

The church is being built by apostles and prophets—they are the foundation (see Ephesians 2:20). It also takes shepherds, evangelists, and teachers, but we have had those all along. Lately, the gift of prophecy is being restored and we can see how God is putting His wisdom into men and women. Through the prophetic word, God has revealed His Father's heart once again for us to behold. What is still missing today is the apostolic.

We do not need "great" apostles. God is interested in apostles of the Lamb, men and women wearing the gray, unappealing coat of humility that Rick Joyner received as he approached the throne of God in His astounding vision in *The Final Quest*. Clothed in humility, they will appear and bow before congregations to wash people's feet. They will hold up lamps and pick up the broken pieces. They will cry with congregations, as well as comfort and encourage them.

Paul saw his own ministry from this perspective as he explained to the Thessalonians: **"But we proved to be gentle among you, as a nursing mother tenderly cares for her own children."** He also wrote, **"Having so fond an affection for you, we were well-pleased to impart to you not only the gospel of God, but also our own lives, because you had become very dear to us" (I Thessalonians 2:7-8 NAS updated).** Those are the kind of apostles we need, rather than the "big shots" coming along to tell us what is going on. We need the apostles of the Lamb, individuals that God will choose and set apart. We are unable to recognize these apostles from a merely human point of view. Like David, these people may still be out in a field, but God will appoint these men and women for the ministry.

The Apostolic Church

There are some churches called apostolic churches. We will not only be prophetic churches, but we will eventually become apostolic churches as well. The five-fold ministry that the Bible talks about in Ephesians 4:11 is not limited to a few individuals, it really is a reflection of the entire church. A church is by nature apostolic, prophetic, evangelistic, and pastoral. It is instructed by the Holy Spirit and it shares words of divine wisdom with others. This ministry is not confined to a few select people; it is a natural expression of the church of Jesus Christ as a whole.

In our times, God is restoring the apostolic within the church. Although we have the "apostolic creed," we cannot even find the word "apostolic" in it. It says: "I believe in a holy, Christian (literally 'catholic', meaning 'universal') church." In the Nicean creed from the fourth century, however, it clearly says: "I believe in a holy, catholic and apostolic church." The apostolic is one of the characteristics of Jesus Himself and He is depositing it into the church today.

Hallmarks of an Apostolic Church: Justified Through the Blood of Jesus

An apostolic church consists of sinners who have been justified through the blood of Jesus. Many of our churches today no longer have sinners in them, but instead people who have "made it" and who are basically well off. These churches become gathering places of the middle class, where sinners no longer feel welcome. An apostolic church is tested for its authenticity every time a sinner walks in, bringing all his garbage with him. Will he feel accepted there?

Being an apostolic church also means that we no longer have to sin. We are being cleansed and sanctified by Jesus, receiving a special kind of purity from Him. Only among pure people will sinners really feel accepted. Why did sinners like to hang out with Jesus? Because He was pure and without sin. In His purity, He did not focus on the sin in others, but He saw them with God's eyes of compassion. Seeing them through His Father's eyes, He was able to recognize beforehand how the Father would later transform them. As long as we are living in bondage to sin, we are forced to always see the sin in others.

When I was working as a painter, I could never enter a room without seeing where paint was chipping off the walls. Whenever I saw the peak of a roof, I immediately noticed whether or not it needed to be completely stripped, primed, and repainted in order to restore it. I was looking at things with a painter's eyes. If you are living in sin, you will always see the sin in other people.

If you are pure and holy through Jesus, you will no longer have that faultfinding way of looking at people, which causes you to notice right away whenever somebody needs counseling in a certain area. You will not even think about what needs to be done to get things in order in a person's life. Instead you will see every individual with the eyes of Jesus. You will be open and welcoming, saying, "Good to have you! You are accepted here, just as you are. We are so glad that you have come!" This will be your attitude even before that person takes a bath.

Father

A Fellowship that Welcomes Sinners

An apostolic church welcomes sinners because all of its members know deep in their hearts that they themselves have only been saved by grace. Paul was so aware of this fact that he could honestly say, "I am the worst of all sinners" (see I Timothy 1:15). He was one of the foremost apostles because he never forgot that he was saved by grace. Others did not need to feel bad when they met Paul. Look at the church in Corinth: It was such a mess! And yet Paul declared at the onset of his letter: **"I always thank God for you because of his grace given you in Christ Jesus" (I Corinthians 1:4).** He was able to make such a statement even though someone in that church was sleeping with his mother-in-law. Paul, however, had a pure heart. He did not have to focus on sin. He saw everything that God had deposited into the people and what He had in mind for them.

It is a hallmark of apostolic churches to make people who drop in from the outside feel comfortable. They just know, "I am welcome in this place. I can let down my guard here because I am accepted." They feel they can mess up without leaders giving them those probing looks, questioning, "How long will it take you to stop that behavior? We've done so much counseling and praying with you. Was all of that in vain?" Instead they repeatedly hear, "I always thank God for you!"

More Love

An apostolic church is a church that has more love. After having so marvelously expounded in I Corinthians 12 on the gifts of the Spirit, those awesome gifts the Lord provides for building His church, Paul said, **"And I show you a still more excellent way" (I Corinthians 12:31 NAS).** In Chapter 13, we read that the more excellent way is love; the passionate love we have above all for God, our Father, but also love for our brothers and sisters. As an apostolic church, we will not be marked by a soulish kind of love, but by the love of the Father and of the Son flowing through us.

Love does not mean that a church has to satisfy everybody's needs and desires. Only infants are constantly fed and cleaned and put in diapers. There comes a time for every one of us to stand before God on our own, searching Him, reading the Bible, and pouring out our hearts before the Lord. We are caught up in a misconception if we expect the church to provide all-inclusive service packages for us. It was never intended to be that way.

A church should be a place where we can find a family of brothers, sisters, and friends—a place to feel at home. That is what we need! God created the fellowship of saints to offer us protection. Even Jesus needed the protection of His disciples. For this reason, He said, **"Greater love has no one than this, that he lay down his life for his friends" (John 15:13).** That sacrificial dimension of love is a whole new aspect. We cannot say, "I love God," and refuse to love our neighbor.

A Family

I believe the secret of the coming power of the body of Christ will be the fruit of the investments that we are making in our spiritual families. These families are not only our churches, but also our prayer groups, our home groups, and the other small groups we are involved in. If we invest in the people that are spiritually close to us, these gatherings can become shelters to us. Think of when Jesus' mother and brothers were standing outside, demanding to see Him. Jesus stood up and looked at His disciples, this tiny band of people who had left their nets, their tollbooths, and their families to embark on the adventure of building the kingdom of God with Him. He looked at them one by one and said, **"for whoever does the will of My Father in heaven is my brother and sister and mother" (Matthew 12:50).**

Earlier in my life, I dearly loved my ministry as a pastor. I went through a deep process of dying to myself when I had to let go of it. Today, I am part of a small community coming together on a regular basis. We have small teams working in different areas of ministry, and we share our lives with one another. I am always deeply moved when I see these people, still walking with me and sharing my life. Allow God to open your eyes to the wonderful grace that He has provided the people who stay with you on the journey. On this risky path, we should never take Christian fellowship for granted. Let us receive God's love and see each other through His eyes of love and compassion.

I think of our little "Schleife" fellowship. Some of us have been walking together for more than twenty years now. Over these years, I have become more acquainted with my own heart. It takes a long time until you no longer perceive each other as pastor or deacon, until you have become close friends who can weep together. Looking back, I am so grateful to God that we did not just quit at some point, but learned to see each other with God's eyes.

Frailty and Brokenness

Another hallmark of an apostolic church is frailty and brokenness. We have had enough "power churches." Today we need churches that carry the gray "mantle of humility," filled with the awesome power of God. Their tremendous achievements are results of their frailty, meekness, and humility. Apostolic churches are commissioned to minister in the body of Christ.

Our Priestly Function as Purifying Agents

Apostolic churches are like a giant liver, cleansing the body of Christ from toxic substances that are circulating in the blood stream, including negative rumors, slander, and pain. As priests, we should take these troubles and burdens to God. It is the job of a priest to bring the offering of frankincense before God and to burn everything that is negative. As priestly, apostolic churches, we must keep coming to the altar, burning what needs to be burnt in the fire of our prayers. Together with other churches, we detoxify the body of Christ from the circulating poison. Over and over, our prayer will be: "Purify our lips! Help us to be a priestly people! We want to be Your priests, oh God!" What else do we need to do? We will not spread anything negative about other churches, not even the headlines. If a church is not doing well, we should take the pain and burden to our God in prayer. It is not an option to spread the news, but it is an opportunity for us to bless that church, to visit and comfort them, and to help rebuild what is broken. Because they know the place of brokenness, apostolic churches will engage in the ministry of encouragement, of comfort, and of hidden intercession for their brothers and sisters. Rivers of living water flow from churches like these.

More Suffering

A third characteristic of apostolic churches is suffering. Paul said, "**...I bear on my body the marks of Jesus**" (**Galatians**

6:17). Another time, Paul prayed, "I want to know Christ and the power of his resurrection and the fellowship of sharing in His sufferings..." (Philippians 3:10). Spiritual anointing cannot be separated from the fellowship of the sufferings of Jesus. Anointing does not just rain down from heaven. When we seek fellowship with the heart of Jesus, we will also have fellowship with His awesome power and anointing.

Prayer

Father, we want to become a kind of church that functions like a liver in Your body, absorbing and excreting toxic substances so the gospel of Your kingdom, Your compassion, and Your restoring mercy and love can flow through us to others. We honor You for this privilege. We pray that You would purify our lips and our hearts in an even deeper way. We pray: Holy Spirit, be like a fire in us that burns everything. Be a threefold filter for our lips that protects us from spreading more poison in Your body. Help us to be the kind of people Paul talked about, focusing only on whatever is pleasing, noble, righteous, true, and whatever builds up. Whatever is good, noble, true, righteous, and well pleasing—these are the things we ought to speak! Thank You, Jesus, that You will bring forth and strengthen the apostolic churches within Your body.

FOURTEEN

My Father Is Greater than All

Living by the Power of God

Two recent incidents have made a deep impression on me. The first one was encountering a woman who had lived a very messed up life for a long time, but who had found new life through the grace of God. One day she heard the cries of an animal by the roadside. When she followed the sound, she found a tiny, little kitten still blind and totally helpless, who had been taken away from its mother. This lady, with her troubled past, took the little cat with her. When I met her, she was carrying it with her in a little box wherever she went. Every two to three hours she had to feed the newborn with a bottle. That picture stuck with me—this tiny little creature in the woman's hand, playfully waving its paws around the bottle, while the woman was trying to stuff the nipple of the bottle into its tiny mouth.

It reminded me of the time when I had fed my own sons and their little fingers fumbled around the bottle. It was a picture of total security and acceptance and of happiness and contentment. It was a powerful analogy—that helpless little kitten with its tiny paws, oozing with pleasure just like a little human being.

Father

To me it was a prophetic sign. We may say, "Oh that was just a cat," but actually it is the expression of total helplessness and frailty that we all experience on this planet. Everything on earth is being shaken; nothing that used to provide us with a sense of security and tradition remains in place.

Even though we may try to put up protective walls here and there, I am convinced that deep down in our hearts we are uneasy and worried about what is going to happen. Just take a walk through an average residential area. It is amazing how many houses are equipped with security systems, light barriers, and other kinds of fancy equipment. Human beings are in desperate need of a safe and protected environment, regardless of who they are or what age group they belong to. Each and every one of us knows about those fears. Even Jesus said in the Garden of Gethsemane: **"My soul is overwhelmed with sorrow to the point of death..." (Matthew 26:38).** In one of His farewell discourses, He said to His disciples: "**...In this world you will have trouble. But take heart! I have overcome the world"** (John 16:33).

The second instance was an encounter I had with a Maori, a member of the native people of New Zealand. The history of rejection that his people have suffered was literally engraved into his facial features. If you have ever seen such a face, you would never be able to forget it, just like the faces of our Jewish or Arab brothers reflect hundreds and thousands of years of history. This Maori had come to know the Lord and he told me about his faith. Then he sang a song to me that he had picked up somewhere. The song puts the deepest cry of the human heart into words and expresses what can ultimately give us rest:

My Father Is Greater Than All

I have a Maker, He formed my heart
Even before time began, my life was in His hands
He knows my name, He knows my every need
He sees each tear as it falls and hears me when I call.
I have a Father, He calls me His own
He'll never leave me no matter where I go
He knows my name; He knows my every need
He sees each tear as it falls
And hears me when I call, and hears when I call.

Something of the secret of the Fatherhood of our God is reflected in that Maori's song. It's a kind of Fatherhood that is foreign to us; it reaches deep down to the core of our being. None of us knows who our heavenly Father really is. We live on memories, on our learning experiences, our internalized images that we hand down from one generation to the next, many of which are religious in nature. Only Jesus gave us a true revelation of the Father. He brought to us the **"true Father,"** as Luther put it in his German translation of Ephesians 3:15. Let us listen to "the true Father over all those who are called children in heaven and on earth." He brought to us the **"Eternal Father."** You will never know who He is unless you see His character reflected in the person of Jesus Christ.

The Father Hears Our Cries

It is part of the eternal character of the Father to hear the cries of those He has created. Whenever people cry out, God will answer. He will even answer in the most desperate situations, when we have gotten ourselves into a total mess and we are convinced that there is no way for God to begin something new in our lives. When we cry out, God will answer. Just read the Jewish books of history in the Bible. Every time they turned to God, He answered them. He will do the same thing today.

One day, a friend called me, telling me that a lawyer had come to his church on Sunday to evaluate for himself what the church looked like these days. He had been raised in an atheist home. During the service, the Holy Spirit gave him a revelation of God's character, but because he had spent all of his life apart from God, he remained uncertain. So he cried out, "God, I know that all this is true, but I just need a sign from You that You are the living God!" What do you think happened?

Early in the morning—it was around four o'clock I think— Jesus came into this man's room. The room was filled with light and Jesus revealed Himself. My friend coerced this man, "What was it like? Tell me more! Just tell me more!" He answered, "I cannot describe it. It was like hundreds and hundreds of crystal clear words raining all over me." Do we see the parallel? It matches the description the seer John gave us in Revelation 1:15: **"his voice was like the sound of rushing waters."** This is our heavenly Father. It is His heart, a true Father's heart. Whenever a child cries out, the father will answer. If we cry out, God will answer us, because that is His character.

We have too many little ideas of who God is, but Jesus came to restore the true picture of the Father. He said, **"...My Father... is greater than all..."** (John 10:29). Our Father is the One who rules, not only in the church, but indeed in heaven and earth. Most of us would accept it as a fact that God is ruling within Christian movements, churches, groups, or whatever we want to call them. God, however, is greater than all.

My Father Is Greater Than All

The whole earth is His property. He appoints kings and He dismisses them. He restores to us a fresh sense of dignity and raises us up from the dust to become like Him. He is the One who created heaven and earth. Why did He do that? Because He wanted to show all of us little creatures that are lying in His hands, like the baby cat I mentioned earlier: "See, I am greater than all, greater than anybody or anything else." Can we believe that God went to such lengths that He actually created an awesome universe just for a few billion humans? For hundreds of years, people have been wondering: "It cannot be just for us. There has got to be more than just one inhabited planet!" But it really is all for us! It really is! Through His creation, God wanted to communicate to us: "I am greater than all!"

When I was standing under the starry sky one night, full of inner turmoil, I suddenly saw a shooting star whizzing right over me. Never before in my life had I seen such a bright, shooting star. It was like a comet with a glowing tail. I could almost hear a whooshing sound above me. That moment I knew: "That's my Fathers' personality." Just like we will strike a match in the darkness to light things up a little, He strikes a match to light a star, only to show a little human like me: "I am the Light, do not be afraid. I am with you." Do we understand that?

It is for the sake of you and me that creation is such a marvelous reflection of the awesome power of our God. Over a long period of time, we kept belittling God, until finally He fit into our churches and preconceived ideas. But our God bursts out of every precast mold. He is the Creator, much greater than even the vast universe. He gave us creation to demonstrate to us beyond any doubt: "My child, My son, My daughter, believe that I am greater than all!"

Father

Why Did God Keep Dealing with Man?

Why do you think God sent Abraham on his long journey—
this seasoned man who had grown rich in his home country, to
a point where he possessed countless herds and scores of
employees? Why did He choose to let this honorable man, who
was to be the father of nations and the father of the faith, live the
life of a nomad? Why on earth would God do something like
that? He did it in order to demonstrate His might to him.

Once you are living on the streets with a backpack on
your back, you will get to know the power of God in a far more
tangible way than ever before—in sandstorms, on cold dark
nights, in the raging of the elements, in thunderstorms and
hail, in cold wet seasons, and then again in the scorching heat of
summer. During those times when he had to fix his eyes upon
the awesome God who had taken him by the hand and led him
out of his comfort zone, saying, **"Look up at the heavens..."**
(Genesis 15:5), something in his heart grew firm. For this very
reason, he was able to take his son and go up to Mount Moriah,
which later became the Temple Mountain in Jerusalem. He laid
him down and told God, "Here he is. You are even greater than
the sacrifice of my son. You are the God who brings the dead
back to life."

And why would God lead the slaves out of Egypt into the
desert? He wanted to demonstrate His power and majesty,
feeding them for forty years in the wilderness. Up to this day,
part of that knowledge seems to be alive in the Jewish people:
God is with us in the desert. How else could they have managed
to cultivate their country? How else could they have made those
arid places fruitful, like they did under David Ben Gurion

and others? Deep within them is the knowledge of a God who is greater than all, who appointed them to be a light for the nations and their temple to be a house of prayer for the nations.

Why was Jesus in Nazareth for thirty years? During that time He was submitted to His parents, serving His family. Part of His reality as a human being was living in the city of Nazareth, out of which nothing good could ever come, among petty little merchants, people talking behind each others backs, and all the other typical attributes of life in a small town. During this same period of His life, Jesus took time to seek His Father. I am convinced that He spent a lot of time in the hills, talking to His heavenly Father. For this reason, He kept going up into the hills. During those days, the knowledge grew in Him: "God is greater than all! He really is greater than all!"

And do you remember how God dealt with His faithful servant Job, when he was sitting among the ashes, scraping his sores with a piece of pottery? His whole family had been destroyed; everything that he ever had was gone and even his friends had turned their backs on him.

But then God showed up! He did not give Job a theological lecture; He demonstrated to him what He was really like. He came with thunder and lightning, and directed Job's attention away from the constant scratching of his sores unto Orion, unto the Pleiades, onto the clouds that carry rain and release it again. God asked him: "Did I not create the horse with all of its strength and its beautiful flowing mane? Did I not create the ostrich that outruns even horse and rider? Is it not I who created the crocodile and the hippo? Look at its strength!" Finally Job put his face in the dust and declared, **"Surely I spoke of things**

**I did not understand, things too wonderful for me to know"
(Job 42:3).**

One thing I know: When Jesus transforms our lives, we will see creation with new eyes and start blessing it once again. What a great privilege the Lord gave the German people, for instance, in the beauty of their land. Whenever I cross the border coming from Switzerland, I feel like my heart can move out into a wide-open space. I just love those faraway horizons. You are able to see the beautiful skies and get a glorious sense of freedom in God, of whom it says in Psalm 31:8, **"You...have set my feet in a spacious place."** God will set our feet on spacious ground.

The Lamb of God—the Greatest Revelation of God's Power

There is one last thing that remains to be said. The power of God, who is greater than all, was revealed even more fully in Jesus Christ, the Lamb of God. He is the greatest revelation of the power of God. John the Baptist pointed to Jesus and said, **"Look, the Lamb of God, who takes away the sin of the world"
(John 1:29).**

In Jesus, the power of God's unconditional love broke into this world—a kind of love that always protects, always trusts, always hopes, always perseveres. It brings reconciliation wherever it goes, through the blood and the power of Jesus— breaking every wall, every iron bolt, and every closed door, being saturated with the meekness, humility, and passion of our God. Through the Lamb the power of God was revealed to its greatest extent. As He was sacrificed on the cross, Jesus became the ransom for our sin. Like a lamb, He did not open His mouth before His shearers. Instead He said, *"Father, receive the offering of My life as a fragrance in favor of My brothers and sisters!"* At the cross, He reconciled this world with His Father.

He hung on the cross, bearing the sin and the curse of the entire world. By doing so, He literally turned the world upside down, paying the price to restore it to God and to create a new mankind. When He cried out, **"It is finished!" (John 19:30)**, it was the birth cry of the new earth. The criminal on His side said: **"Jesus, remember me when you come into your** [Father's] **kingdom!"** Jesus answered him right there on the cross, **"... today, you will be with Me in paradise" (Luke 23:42-43).** Thus Jesus brought the first fruit of a new mankind, a saved criminal, to His Father in paradise. This is the tremendous power of the love of God Jesus talked about, when He told us: If I can fill you with that love, nothing will be impossible to you. Love is stronger than death. **"It always protects, always trusts, always hopes, always perseveres. Love never fails... " (I Corinthians 13:7-8).** It is the **"most excellent way" (I Corinthians 12:31)** that Paul wrote about. It is the way that reaches far beyond the gifts of the Spirit and accomplishes far greater things.

The greatest gift is Jesus Himself; through Him, the passionate love and mercy of God came into the world. Only this kind of love enables us to turn the other cheek when someone strikes us. It enables us to give our cloak to the person who previously took our tunic and to go a second mile with someone who already forced the first mile on us. We will be able to love our enemies not only theoretically, but also truly in our hearts, heaping fiery coals upon their heads, searching their well-being, reaching out to them before they do harm to us. We will show them that they are loved and chosen by God.

Father

What a tremendous power is found in the Lamb! I am convinced that we are just about to enter the time for that power of the Lamb to be fully revealed. According to the Revelation of John, no one in heaven, on earth, or under the earth has the power to break the seals, except for the Lamb of God (see Revelation 5). Now is the time for the rulership of the Lamb to begin—over this world, over the nations of the world, and over the structures of society. The time has come for the seals to be broken and for us to experience the awesome power of the Lamb. It is even time for the wrath of the Lamb to be unleashed, a time when people will be restrained and kept from entering into the kingdom of God and when the keys of revelation will be withheld from them.

The Power Lives in You!

What an awesome power is in the Lamb! For this reason Count Zinzendorf's Moravians had a picture of the Lamb on their seal. They overcame in the power of the Lamb. Under this sign, they went out on the mission field, to the nations. Under this sign, they built cities and founded schools. Under the sign of the Lamb, they advanced the kingdom of God in the world, everywhere on every continent.

In Herrnhut, something of the New Jerusalem was birthed. Everyone was being taken care of—the widows, the single men, the world—everyone and everything had its place. There was an all-encompassing vision of the world, under the sign of the Lamb and His love that **"always protects, always trusts, always hopes, always perseveres" (I Corinthians 13:7).**

This love is alive in you if you have accepted Jesus Christ. His very passion is alive in you. You have the same power in you that was in Daniel, when he stood in the lions' den and the angels kept the lions' mouths shut for one night. This same power was alive in the men who were thrown in the fiery furnace. The same power was alive in Paul Schneider, "the Preacher from Buchenwald," who kept yelling Bible verses out of his little starving-cell at the Nazi death camp. He wanted everyone to hear it until he was finally silenced.

The same power lives inside of you. It is a power that conquers cities, as happened during the Azusa Street revival in the early twentieth century in the desolate city of Los Angeles. The outpouring of the Holy Spirit began when two men, filled with the passion of God declared, "We'd rather be dead than to live on without a revival!"

Back then, many thought these people were going too far. But they did not. It was plainly the power of the Lamb within them, saying, "We will not rest until the presence of God has come among us." It was the power of the Lamb that proclaimed, "God wants to draw the world back into His Father's house."

God is Greater Than Our Hearts

"...God is greater than our hearts" (I John 3:20). He really is greater than our hearts. We know that our hearts are a constant source of danger to us because the human heart is so full of deceit. It will always try to trim down God, reducing Him to our own ideas, limiting Him to what we feel, or what seems right to us at a given moment. However, **"God is greater than our hearts."** You will never be able to flow in the power of the Holy Spirit unless you know that God is greater than your heart. We are hampering the kingdom of God if we do not allow God to be greater than our hearts—whatever may be in our hearts.

Father

God needs men and women who are willing to be bold and courageous today. We need to have the "paresia," the audacity of the Holy Spirit in us that gives us the freedom to dare to do things, and even to make mistakes and to mess up. God does not want perfectionism. In fact, He hates it. Perfectionism was invented by the devil to cloud the character of God—it is a total eclipse. Jesus came to us as a Man full of frailty. He felt hunger and thirst. He let us share His very heart. He wept over cities. He laughed with tax collectors and sinners. Jesus wants to set us free to a new lifestyle of freedom in the Spirit.

Oftentimes, we act like know-it-alls toward our brothers and sisters at the front lines who dared to set out and do something, and sometimes that is our attitude even toward leaders or movements in the church. We cannot afford such a mindset any longer. Whoever dares to step out and take risks will surely mess up from time to time. For this very reason, we are to function as a body of believers.

If one of us stumbles or falls, we can admonish each other with love and meekness, putting our arms around each other, saying, "Brother, don't you think your actions might have been a little out of place?" It is our obligation to help one another get back on our feet. Let me make one thing very clear: If you have given your heart to God, He is for you. He is on your side fighting for you!

David Strengthened Himself in the Lord

Let us remember David once again. David truly was a man of God. Yet, every man of God will have certain days every once in a while, where he blows a fuse and acts out of his own understanding. When Saul persecuted David for an extended period of time, he said to himself: "That's it, I'll go and take shelter with the Philistines." What kind of shelter did he get there? One of the Philistine kings gave a city to David and his six hundred men with all of their families. He was allowed to set up his camp there and venture out on his campaigns.

Finally, he was asked to join the Philistines in battle against Israel. Fortunately, the other Philistine rulers became angry and had him sent back. When he returned to Ziklag, the city was burnt and the Amalekites had robbed them of all the women and children, as well as their possessions. Do you see what had happened? David had followed his own will without asking God (see I Samuel 27). He thought they would be safe with the Philistines, but instead their city was burned and he was almost stoned to death by his own friends.

I am fascinated by David's reaction to this crisis. He did not submerge into heavy self-accusation, scolding himself, "If only I had done this or that! If only I had stayed in the desert!" Instead he went to God, asking, "God, what shall I do now?" In the biblical account it says, **"But David strengthened himself in the Lord his God" (I Samuel 30:6 NAS)**. And what a God He is!

David found courage in the "God who is greater than all," (see Psalm 135:5) in the Lord who was greater than their burnt-down city and even greater than their kidnapped women and children. He is infinitely greater than every circumstance. He strengthened himself in the Lord, not looking at his infuriated friends who were raging with angry reproaches, accusing him, "What a stupid idea! Why did you make us live among the Philistines?" After he had strengthened himself in the Lord, God told him, "Go after those Amalekites." On top of everything, two hundred of his six hundred men grew tired on the way. Yet God was with him and everything was restored to them. The spoils were so abundant that David could use them as gifts to the elders of the tribe of Judah to establish his future kingdom.

We need to know the Father. Only then can we live and take our stand on the secure foundation of His Fatherhood. Without this foundation, our Spirit will not be free to receive whatever God wants to do through you and me. The foundation of God's Fatherhood is a safe place, safe enough to sleep through a life-threatening storm, like Jesus did. When they woke Him up, He simply said, "Why are you guys making such a commotion? My Father is greater than all." This is the security we all need as well.

The Army of God

We will become an army for our God. We will rise up and march into the world to reclaim it. This army will restore what has been stolen. There is so much to be reclaimed; in the name of Jesus and for the glory of our God we will do it.

Let me requote that famous saying of the Quakers: "Christians are incredibly happy, absolutely fearless, and always in trouble." I can testify to that fact from my own experience. It is incredible happiness to be a son of the awesome Father God who is greater than all, and to be a friend and brother of Jesus, who is the firstborn. It is a tremendous, rejuvenating power that keeps filling and fueling our lives. We will be incredibly happy, even in the midst of difficulties. And we are always in trouble—but thank God because we need those troublesome situations to experience God and to grow our roots deeper and deeper into the Father's heart. If we are not yet absolutely fearless, we are at least on our way toward that goal and we will reach it because we personally know our God who lives in our hearts. We have the authority and the anointing of the Father and His love that is stronger than death.

Prayer

Eternal Father, Father of our Lord Jesus Christ and through Him our very own Father, we want to give You and Your Son who took possession of His inheritance praise, honor, and power.

Father, I rebuke all fatherlessness, wherever people have been cheated by their role models. Those role models were false fathers, only causing hurt and disappointment. Even we as leaders in the church are guilty of being false fathers. Father, in the name of Jesus I rebuke the power of the hurt and fatherlessness. We also declare that you, Lucifer, have no power over mankind anymore. We have been purchased to be children of our heavenly Father, to be His sons and daughters whom He passionately loves.

Father, we cry out to You as Your children. We cry, "Abba, Father; Abba, Father; Abba, Father; have mercy on us!" Have mercy on our marriages and on our children; have mercy on us who are fathers ourselves. Have mercy on our governments, have mercy on our nations. May they become nations where Your way of Fatherhood is being practiced.

I bless you with the Spirit of Fatherhood. May He "brood" over you who are a hungry, thirsty, and searching people. May you be ready to go after the Father through Jesus Christ and to be satisfied by Him. Again, I pronounce this word over every one of you: The Father is greater than all.

Amen!